Generating Prose

Generating Prose

Relations, Patterns, Structures

Willis L. Pitkin, Jr.

Utah State University

MACMILLAN PUBLISHING COMPANY

New York

Macmillan Publishing Company
866 Third Avenue, New York, New York 10022

Collier Macmillan Canada, Inc.

Library of Congress Cataloging-in-Publication Data
Pitkin, Willis L., Jr.
    Generating prose.

    Includes index.
    1. English language—Rhetoric. I. Title.
PE1408.P54 1987   808'.042   86–10410
ISBN 0–02–395560–0

Printing: 1   2   3   4   5   6   7   Year: 7   8   9   0   1   2   3

ISBN   0-02-395560-0

To my parents and my children.

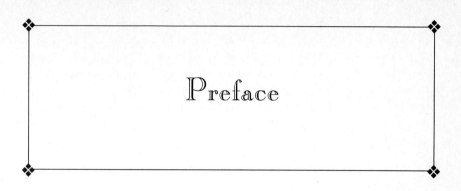

Preface

A text that departs as radically as this one does from what composition teachers are used to—if not entirely satisfied with—needs explaining and justifying. Let me first explain what this text is not.

Obviously it is not a traditional rhetoric, a handbook, or a reader. Nor, despite superficial resemblances, does it fit neatly in the newer category of what are called "sentence combining" texts.

Generating Prose is an attempt to teach what we might call the grammar of ideas—the basic code that enables human beings to put utterances together. It is based on the conviction—illustrated by the DNA code in genetic evolution and by the laws of physics in the evolution of our universe—that the richest expressions of complex information trace to simple rules applied recursively.

This sounds technical (although it finds clear and compelling expression in Jeremy Campbell's *Grammatical Man*.) But *Generating Prose* is not a technically complex book. It is structured in three parts, focusing in turn on (1) the ways pairs of assertions can relate to one another, (2) the patterns these relations take as we increase the number of assertions, and (3) the syntactic options available for packaging those patterns. Following, in more detail, is the format of *Generating Prose*.

Part I (**Relations**) sets down the "primitives" of discourse—the ways any two assertions can relate logically. Structure is not an issue here (although each relation may be presented in a variety of syntactic structures). What is done here is to define the set of discourse relations: cause/effect (*because x y*, etc.), includer/included (*x for example y*, etc.), coordinate/coordinate (*x or y*, etc.), and so on. And in Part I these relations are examined one at a time, as paired units, rather than as constituents of complex discourse.

Part II (**Patterns**) builds on this "linear" taxonomy by combining ("chunking") these relations in hierarchical patterns. For instance, given the relations *x so y* (cause/effect) and *x for example y* (includer/included), we might form this hierarchical pattern.

		so	
	x		*y*
for example			
x	*y*		
We had helped them on various occasions	We had tended their dog when they went to Atlantic City		They had us over for dinner

The same two relations, arranged in another hierarchical pattern, might yield:

so			
x	*y*		
	for example		
	x		*y*
We had helped them on various occasions	They repaid us in several ways		They had us over for dinner

In Part II the hierarchical patterns involve manipulating entire independent clauses ("full assertions," as they are called at this point). The purpose is to allow the experimenting writer to construct hierarchical patterns of discourse without worrying about syntax. In essence he or she is learning to write paragraphs before learning to write multilevel sentences, which is as it should be: it is *easier* to arrange grammatically independent assertions in coherent paragraphs than to collapse them into a multilevel sentence with, say, a single base clause and several free modifiers. We know it is easier because little children can string single assertions coherently before they can construct a complex sentence of such a string.

Part III (**Structures**) attacks in three stages the issues of syntactic patterns. Stages one and two introduce structures of coordination and structures of subordination. (These are not Francis Christensen's categories, a blend of the semantic, the syntactic, and the rhetorical; rather, these are purely syntactic categories, grammatical structures.)

Having practiced the various *discourse* relations and patterns, the student is ready to examine *syntactic* structures—to combine, say,

		so	
	x		*y*
for example			
x	*y*		
We had helped them on various occasions	We had tended their dog when they went to Atlantic City		They had us over for dinner

into such a structures as this:

    A. We had helped on various occasions—tending their dog, for example, when they went to Atlantic City—so they had us over for dinner.

Or this:

    B. Because we had helped them on various occasions (such as tending their dog when they went to Atlantic City), they had us over for dinner.

Stage three of **Structures**—"Structures of Expansion"—deals with the grammatical shapes possible *within* the base clause, largely through expanding noun phrases, verb phrases, and adjective phrases by means of restrictive modification and through filling the basic noun slots with various nominal phrases and clauses (participial, infinitive, relative, included, and so on).

As one who for twenty-seven years has taught students to write, I recognize a major concern that teachers riffling these pages might have: exercises abound, and if one were to require these exercises in addition to a theme each week, the reading load (they think) would be staggering.

Good news! *Generating Prose* is designed to accomplish much in little time. Used the way it's intended, this text will actually lessen the reading load, considerably. But this requires that (1) the exercises be the main teaching tool, and (2) the weekly themes be read largely as an index of how well particular exercises have taken.

For teachers whose practice it has been to assign full-length themes and mark everything every time, this new tack may seem suspect. If "trust me" isn't enough, perhaps an analogy might help. Assigning a weekly theme to inexperienced writers and marking all their errors is like assigning a Mozart sonata to beginning piano students and rapping their wrists for every false note and faulty rest. Such a tactic teaches chiefly despair. Successful piano teachers bring their students along gradually, through finger exercises, working slowly up to simple pieces, finally to major works. *Generating Prose* is a book largely of discourse finger exercises and simple pieces.

In other words, I'm suggesting that the theme-a-week teacher (and I remain one) look upon the daily exercises as the true vehicle for teaching the basic principles of writing and upon the theme as a test of how well all of those principles are coming along at any given point. Treated in this fashion, the exercises will provide instant and precisely focused feedback on the student's mastery of basic discourse principles, and the weekly (or occasional) theme will provide a holistic view of his or her general progress. This approach actually lessens one's reading and grading time—less than a minute each on most of the exercises, perhaps five minutes on the weekly theme. Most important, *it teaches principles that actually make improvements in our students' writing.*

It's impossible to say where and when all the seeds that became *Generating Prose* were sown. Since my beloved parents are both gifted in their use of language and played language with me even more than they played blocks or cars, at least some of the seeds came from flowerings before I was born. And of course my formal education, in that I was a typical middle-class Anglo of mid-twentieth-century America, was nurtured by a rich rhetorical tradition with roots many hundreds of years deep. But if I were to hazard as precise a source as possible for this text, I would say that the "fair seed time" was the decade from the fall of 1957 through the spring of 1966—from my first undergraduate classes with Francis Christensen, at the University of Southern California, to my last shared teaching duties with Albert Upton, at Whittier College. That the intervening twenty years have yielded but a modest harvest says less about the seeds than about the soil they fell on.

Christensen, who sixteen years after his death still exerts an influence on the teaching of composition disproportionate to the volume (although not to the merit) of his written work, introduced me to discourse structure. My own model of discourse structure, the model that informs this text, departs from his in major ways, yet it took a decade of tinkering with Christensen's structures of subordination and coordination to bring me, in 1968, to formulate the present model.

And during the last three years of that decade my tinkering had the added perspective of Albert Upton's marvelously clear taxonomy of semantic functions, all of which found their way into the discourse functions treated in *Generating Prose*. Upton published even less than

Christensen did, yet his "first book in semantics," *Design for Thinking,* says more in less space than perhaps any other book I've read.

To those two mentors (and deeply valued friends) I owe so very much. *Generating Prose* is a heartfelt—if belated and not totally adequate—gesture of gratitude.

I owe a special debt also to a third scholar, George Miller, a man I've met only through his writing. Those who know Miller's research will recognize as his the concept of hierarchical chunking that informs *Generating Prose.* I consider it one of the most powerful pedagogical concepts of our age.

I owe much to others also—so much to so many that I can't begin to acknowledge them all. To the readers that helped me through early versions—Professor Earl B. Brown, Jr. of Radford University, Professor John Clifford of University of North Carolina at Wilmington, Professor Barbara J. Craig at Del Mar College, Professor Richard L. Larson at Herbert H. Lehman College of the City University of New York, Professor Walter E. Meyers of North Carolina State University, and, especially, Professor John Mellon of University of Illinois at Chicago Circle Campus—my gratitude; their advice was welcome and helpful. To Gregory Strachov, whose painting *Northbound* speaks its gentle message from the cover, I say, "Spasibo." That painting and our friendship mean more to me than words can express. To Susan Didrickson Anker, who knew the project would work, and to Vicky Horbovetz, Tucker Jones, Eben W. Ludlow, Sharon Sharp, and Aliza Greenblatt, who made sure it did, I am deeply grateful. To Shelley Hall, indefatigable typist, bless your dancing digits. To Bill Strong, without whom (and without whose word processor) I would still be working on the index, and to Charlotte Wright, who shared with me the task of reading proofs, very special thanks, my very special friends. And to the community of scholars—students and colleagues—I live among, thank you for affording me the good life.

W.L.P.

Note to the Student

W. C. Fields, who is remembered today largely for his comic roles in early films and for his unabashed fondness for alcohol, began his entertainment career as a juggler in vaudeville. As excellent a comic actor as he was, he was an even better juggler, one of the all-time best, at least until alcohol began to ravage his central nervous system. Eyewitness accounts of his early act (he began juggling professionally at age eleven, in 1891) and those occasional juggling segments in his films record his uncanny ability to keep objects in the air—sometimes even after an object, evidently fumbled, had nearly hit the floor, to be captured in the last millisecond by the toe of his shoe and returned to the dazzling dance his hands were performing. If you should ever have the opportunity to watch movie footage of Fields at his juggling, remember this: For every cueball or apple or vase that he successfully returned to the complex cycle vaulting above his head, he probably dropped five hundred or more in those early, painful years of practice.

And painful they were. According to the biographers, Fields's father was a greengrocer, who sold fresh fruit and vegetables from a pushcart; and young Fields used his father's produce to practice his juggling, stealing (and dropping and bruising and splitting and otherwise ruining) the yet-to-be-sold vegetables and fruit at every opportunity. As a reward for his long hours of practice (which, for his father, counted only as ruined produce), Fields's father beat him furiously. W. C. Fields found learning to juggle tough.

So what's the point? Simply this: With this text you will undertake (probably helped by a teacher and several classmates) to learn how to put ideas together into increasingly complex units of coherent discourse—an accomplishment in many ways as challenging as keeping a dozen pieces of fruit in the air for several minutes. W. C.

Fields did not try that first evening beside his father's cart to keep airborne three oranges, a pineapple, two bananas, and half a dozen apples. He probably started with a pair of limes. And he dropped them occasionally—at first quite often.

You will spend most of your time here working up slowly to the task of writing meaningful discourse of any great length. You'll do it by playing games—simple ones at first and then more and more complex ones—with the basic units of discourse. And often enough you'll drop things. But that's how you'll learn what these units can and cannot be made to do.

Don't be afraid to experiment, to make mistakes, to try more than you've been asked to try (and often, therefore, to fail). That's how W. C. Fields became an accomplished juggler of apples and oranges. That's how you are going to become an accomplished juggler of ideas. And no one will beat you for bruising the limes.

W.L.P.

Contents

Introduction   1

PART I Relations   13

PART II Patterns

PART III Structures 113

Generating Prose

Introduction

A high school friend of mine—his name is Al—spent most of one afternoon trying to teach me to drive a golf ball down the middle of a fairway. That was nearly thirty years ago, but the frustration of that afternoon is still fresh. Al, an excellent golfer, drove four or five balls straight out of sight, to show me what to do. Then he helped me position my feet, my head, my shoulders, my hands.

In the next few hours I must have hit three hundred balls, almost all of them hopping a few feet from the tee or slicing weakly onto the next fairway over. Occasionally Al would reposition my feet or hands or would tell me to keep my eye on the ball. And I'd try again, and again the ball would bounce off the tee or curve a short arc to the adjoining fairway.

I'm sure that if just *one* of those three hundred balls I hit had done what Al and I both wanted it to, I'd be an avid golfer today. But none did, and I haven't held a golf club in nearly thirty years.

I begin with this story to let you know that I too, like many of you reading this text, have felt the frustration of trying to learn from an expert and failing miserably. Some of you have probably tried harder and longer to learn to write well than I tried to learn golf, and some of you probably had teachers who wrote even better than Al golfed.

Why should I be confident this book will help students and teachers transact business better than Al and I did so many years back? The reason has to do with a basic fact of teaching that I didn't know then but do now: We learn a complex behavior—whether writing an essay or driving a golf ball—more successfully when our teacher can break that behavior into its stages and sub-stages, its basic units.

This text breaks the complex behavior called "writing coherent discourse"* into its basic units. Then, step by step, you will learn how these basic units can be combined to enable you to write coherent discourse.

In writing this book I have made four assumptions: two about the students who will be using it and two about the way complex discourse is put together.

First, I assume that you already know a great deal more about your language than you think you do. This includes a great deal about what's called its grammar—the relationship of any one "part of speech" to all the others in a sentence. Many of you would deny that you know English grammar, but the fact that you understand the preceding sentence well enough to deny it proves my point.

Still, I'd like for you to prove it to yourself.

Get a piece of paper and a pen or pencil. Then use the twelve words from the following list to make a single sentence. Use *all* the words. Don't use any word twice. Take your time and play with all twelve words until you've put them together in a sequence that makes sense. Please stay with it till you get these twelve words to work together.

1. an	*4.* on	*7.* saw	*10.* two
2. I	*5.* with	*8.* kittens	*11.* large
3. extremely	*6.* man	*9.* lap	*12.* his

Now that you've finished, let's take a moment to appreciate what you were able to do. Perhaps a sentence came to you fairly quickly. Perhaps it came only after you had struggled through several false starts, wishing you had one word more or one word less or one word changed (perhaps *a* for *an*). But at last it all made sense, and you wrote "I saw an extremely large man with two kittens on his lap."†

Here's what I find remarkable, and what convinces me that you know a great deal about the grammar of English:

1. The odds are overwhelming that you had never said, never read, never heard that sentence before. Yet you knew what you were looking for.

---

*The term *discourse* will be defined later. But if you watch how the term is being used, you'll develop a useful definition on your own.

†My students and I have come up with only two other, less likely but still grammatical, possibilities: "On his lap I saw an extremely large man with two kittens" and "An extremely large man with two kittens on his lap saw I."

2. Those twelve words can go together in over 479 *million* possible sequences. Only three that I know of are grammatical.

3. If you had to combine those words in every possible sequence, working at the rate of 1,000 each hour (seventeen each minute, one every 3.5 seconds) ten hours each day, it would take you over 130 *years* to get them all done. But you can find the most grammatical sequence in a matter of minutes.

So either you had incredible luck coming up with that sentence, or you know a great deal about English grammar. You would have difficulty explaining what you know (and so would your teacher, and so would I), but you know it in the way that really counts: you can *use* the knowledge, even if you can't explain it.

This does not mean, of course, that you have nothing more to learn about grammar. Each culture has subpatterns in its grammar, and when patterns conflict, one is usually called superior and the others inferior. Tom Brokaw and Barbara Jordan and N. Scott Momaday and S. I. Hayakawa and Phyllis Schlafly and William Raspberry speak and write a prestige grammar. You may speak and write one that they consider inferior. If you say "I seen him" or "This don't fit" or "That girl she take my wallet," your grammar differs from theirs (and from mine, incidentally). The differences would be completely unimportant except that they will make you the victim of occasional linguistic bigotry. If you want to know at what points your grammar differs from mine or your teacher's, ask your teacher for help or get hold of a good handbook. But whether or not your grammar conflicts in minor ways with mine, we share enough knowledge of English grammar to get some truly important things done in this book.

My second assumption is that a major part of your difficulty with writing has to do with the difficulty you have building ideas. You have trouble "getting started" and "knowing what to say next." Of course you may have difficulty with other matters too—with spelling and punctuation, with choosing the right word, with making a verb agree with its subject ("a *bowl* of apples *was* on the table"). But however important these other difficulties may be (and they are important), the approach we're taking in this book assumes that they are less important than the problem of building ideas. If you haven't built a meaningful idea, it doesn't much matter that you've spelled all your words correctly. So although this book includes exercises that will help you with your spelling, your punctuation, your word choice, and so forth, the focus of every exercise will be on building ideas.

The first and second assumptions have to do with how well prepared you are for this text. The third and fourth assumptions have to do with what I consider to be the structure of coherent discourse—the segments of your writing "golf swing."

The third assumption concerns the most basic units of coherent discourse. Many writing textbooks assume that the basic units will be found within the sentence. So those textbooks focus on the structural parts of the sentence—units with names like "subject," "predicate," "relative clause," and so on. Certainly, as an educated citizen you might well want to know that the sentence "Rhonda was very angry" has a subject (*Rhonda*) and a predicate (*was very angry*) and that the predicate contains the intensifier *very*. But this textbook assumes (remember our first assumption) that you already know how to recognize and use subjects, predicates, and intensifiers and that learning what grammarians name those structural units won't improve your writing very much.

This text looks at a sentence such as "Rhonda was very angry" as a single assertion, a statement of fact that needn't be broken into its grammatical subunits. Instead, in this text we'll be looking to see how an assertion such as "Rhonda was very angry" can *function in discourse*, which is to say *how it can relate to other assertions*. And here is assumption three:

> *The basic units of coherent discourse are the total number of ways any two assertions can relate, a set of basic relations.*

In other words, by itself the assertion "Rhonda was very angry" is not a basic unit of writing. It is only one half of a basic unit. It needs another unit to relate to, and there are only so many ways two units can relate.

Part I of our text details what I consider to be the basic ways two assertions can relate. But let me give you some examples here to let you see the principles our third assumption is defining.

In the following list I have paired the assertion "Rhonda was very angry" with three other assertions. Each time the paired assertions form a relation. And to show you that each relation can be used for other pairs of assertions, I have named the relation and given two or three additional examples.

1. Each of the following paired assertions represents the basic relation cause/effect (or *x therefore y*):
   a. *Ronda was very angry*, so she slammed down the receiver.
   b. Twice he had stood her up. *Rhonda was therefore very angry*.

    c. Because I have a test tomorrow, I'm going to review all my notes.

    d. Their demands having been met, the hijackers released the hostages.

2. Each of the following paired assertions represents the basic relation assertion/intensification (or *x indeed y*):

    a. *Rhonda was very angry.* In fact, she was furious.

    b. Rhonda was upset. In fact, *she was very angry.*

    c. He was often—indeed usually—late for work.

    d. They don't look like sisters. They don't even look like members of the same species.

3. Each of the following paired assertions represents the basic relation contrast/contrast (or *true x yet y*):

    a. Although *Rhonda was very angry*, she remained polite.

    b. We've found the keys, but now we've lost the car.

    c. Even if it's late, I think we should call them.

Before we go on to the fourth assumption, let me point out three important facts about discourse relations. First, notice that different subject matters can use the same relation (Rhonda's anger and the hijackers' demands are entirely different subjects, but both can be involved in a cause/effect relation). Second, notice that "Rhonda was angry" was the *cause* in one cause/effect relation and the *effect* in another, the *assertion* in one assertion/intensification relation and the *intensification* in another. In other words, what determines the function of any assertion is not the assertion itself but *how it relates to another assertion*. Third, notice that the term *assertion* has been used to refer to units that are gramatically different. "Rhonda was very angry" is a full sentence (sometimes called an independent clause), capable of being punctuated as a separate unit. But structures such as "because I have a test tomorrow" and "their demands having been met" and "although Rhonda was very angry" are not full sentences. Still, we're calling anything capable of forming one half of a relationship—whatever its grammatical structure—an assertion. This figures importantly in our fourth (and final) assumption.

The fourth assumption has to do with what happens when we combine more than two assertions at a time. It also has to do with how we process and remember information.

For starters, let's try processing and remembering not a number of assertions but rather a series of letters. Read through the sequence of nineteen letters below, close your book, and see how many you can recall in their proper order:

Q - H - R - M - D - B - N - F - Z - G - U - E - X - F - P - C - Y - J - I

The purpose of asking you to recall a random sequence of nineteen letters was not to humiliate you. The average person can process and remember only six or eight letters in a sequence. But if that is so, how it is that we're expected to process and recall not merely letters but also words, sentences, paragraphs, and whole chapters of books?

Let's see if we can find an answer by trying to process and remember another sequence of nineteen letters. This one should be a great deal easier.

D - E - S - K - L - A - M - P - E - R - A - S - E - R - P - A - P - E - R

If you were able to recall this sequence (or even if you were able to recall, say, the first eight letters or the last eleven), it was because you were remembering not the individual letters but rather groups of letters that spelled words. Instead of having to remember the first four letters separately, you have to remember just one word—*desk*. One word is easier to remember than four letters. A sequence of four words is easier to remember than a sequence of nineteen letters. Because this process of putting several separate pieces of information into one piece is so important to our understanding of how ideas grow, we'll give the process a name. We'll call it "chunking."

Chunking is a process that can go over and over again, at higher and higher levels. For example, when you had to remember the nineteen letters in the last sequence, you might first have chunked them into four words:

(four words)   desk   lamp   eraser   paper

(nineteen letters)
D - E - S - K - L - A - M - P - E - R - A - S - E - R - P - A - P - E - R

But the chunking process needn't stop there. Perhaps you saw that the first two words could stand for *one* chunk of information. A *desk* is one thing and a *lamp* is another. But a *desk lamp* is one thing again. Thus, our four words might make up only three chunks of information:

(three chunks)   desk lamp   eraser   paper

(four chunks)   desk   lamp   eraser   paper

And further chunking is still possible. Perhaps you saw that the three separate items you were remembering—desk lamp, eraser, and paper—might fit in a single category, the category "things I use when I write." Now the three chunks of information make one chunk:

(one chunk)   things I use when I write

(three chunks)   desk lamp   eraser   paper

Don't be confused by the fact that the single chunk at the top level actually contains more words (and more letters) than our original nineteen-letter sequence. It is still only a single chunk of information, only *one* thing to remember. And thus, through successive rechunking of information, it is possible to go from nineteen separate items (far beyond the capacity of our short-term memory) to four items to three to one:

(nineteen chunks)

D - E - S - K - L - A - M - P - E - R - A - S - E - R - P - A - P - E - R

desk   lamp   eraser   paper   (four chunks)

desk lamp   eraser   paper   (three chunks)

things I use when I write   (one chunk)

This process of chunking underlies our fourth assumption. Our fourth assumption is that we build complex ideas not by adding one piece of information to another in a long sequence (like our sequence of nineteen letters) but rather by successively rechunking more and more information. To illustrate again this rather difficult concept, let's try building an idea, a fairly simple one, and see what we find out.

Our idea is going to start with three assertions:

A. It costs too much.
B. It's the wrong color.
C. I'm not going to buy it.

To build an idea from these three assertions, all we need to do is combine them. The question is, how many ways can we combine them and still have them make sense? Part of that question is easy to answer. We can combine the three assertions in six possible sequences: *ABC, ACB, BAC, BCA, CAB,* and *CBA*. But will all six make equal sense?

If building complex ideas is merely a matter of stringing independent assertions in a sequence, then any sequence should do. But if building complex ideas involves rechunking more and more information at higher and higher levels, then some sequences should make sense and others shouldn't. Let's try all six possible sequences (with what we'll be calling "signal" words added—words that signal the relationship of the assertions) and judge for ourselves whether all six make sense:

ABC It costs too much and it's the wrong color so I'm not going to buy it.

ACB It costs too much so I'm not going to buy it and it's the wrong color.

BAC It's the wrong color and it costs too much so I'm not going to buy it.

BCA It's the wrong color so I'm not going to buy it and it costs too much.

CAB I'm not going to buy it because it costs too much and it's the wrong color.

CBA I'm not going to buy it because it's the wrong color and it costs too much.

I feel comfortable with four of these sequences and uncomfortable with two. Do two of them seem to you to be illogical? If you feel that sequences *ACB* and *BCA* (the second and fourth) are somehow out of order, you and I agree. Now the task is to see how chunking might account for what you and I agree is so.

A simple explanation is this. The three assertions actually form *two* chunks at the highest level of organization—a *cause* chunk (or *reason*) and an *effect* chunk (or *result*). In other words, two of the assertions work together as a cause; the other assertion works as the effect. One way to diagram the way they work is this:

	so	
cause (or reason)		effect (or result)
It costs too much and it's the wrong color		I'm not going to buy it

The three assertions relate as two chunks, *x so y*.

But *ABC* wasn't the only sequence that made sense. So did *CAB*. *CAB* simply reverses the order of the two main chunks, putting the *effect* first and the *cause* second (*x because y*):

	because	
effect		cause
I'm not going to buy it		it costs too much and it's the wrong color

That accounts for two of the sequences that make sense: *ABC* and *CAB*. But we had two other sequences that also made sense: *BAC* and *CBA*. How does the concept of chunking help us explain them? All we need to remember is that *chunking can occur level after level*—that we can have chunks within chunks. Let's rediagram our first sequence, showing this time how *A* and *B* relate, as *coordinate* chunks within the *cause* chunk:

	so	
cause		effect
and		
coordinate	coordinate	
It costs too much	it's the wrong color	I'm not going to buy it

And just as the *cause* and *effect* can be reversed, so can these two coordinate chunks. Thus, we get sequence *BAC*:

	so	
cause		effect
and		
coordinate	coordinate	
It's the wrong color	it costs too much	I'm not going to buy it

And we get sequence *CBA*:

	because	
effect		cause
	and	
	coordinate	coordinate
I'm not going to buy it	it's the wrong color	it costs too much

And these four sequences are all we can get as long as the *cause* chunk has two assertions and the *effect* chunk has one. Sequences *ACB* and *BCA*, the two sequences that didn't make sense, split the *cause* chunk in two. It doesn't make sense to give the *cause*, then the *effect*, then another *cause* of the same *effect*.

Introduction Exercise

To reinforce the concept of chunking, see if you can match different meanings of the sequence

extra   heavy   baby   diapers

with the different chunking patterns. Match the number of the meaning with the letter of the diagram representing the chunking pattern of that meaning.

1. diapers for extra-heavy babies
2. baby diapers that are extra heavy
3. extra diapers for heavy babies
4. additional heavy diapers for babies

A.

extra | heavy | baby | diapers

B.

extra | heavy | baby | diapers

C.

extra | heavy | baby | diapers

D.

extra | heavy | baby | diapers

These, then, are the four assumptions this book makes:

1. You already know a great deal about your native language, especially the grammar of that language.
2. A major problem you have with writing is with developing complex ideas.
3. The basic ideas, the basic units of discourse, are the logical relationship between two assertions (two minimal *chunks*).
4. Complex ideas develop when we increase the amount of information (the number of assertions) in related chunks.

If assumptions 3 and 4 still sound very technical, don't worry. They *are* technical. They are my attempt to explain something very complex: how ideas grow. And they are always right here in the Introduction if you want to look at them occasionally to see if they make better sense. But even if they never make better sense to you than they do now, what is important is not whether you can explain what they mean but whether you can learn to use them to improve your writing. And that is what the rest of the book is about.

Part I

Relations

In the Introduction we looked at four assumptions. The first was that you already know a great deal about language, especially grammar. So although you will meet a variety of grammatical structures in this section of the book, you won't be asked to focus on those grammatical structures yet. (In fact, you won't look at grammatical structures at all till Part III, and even then it won't get very technical.)

Assumptions two and three relate directly to this first major section of the book—"Relations." Our second assumption is that your difficulties with writing include, at the most basic level, a difficulty in building ideas. Although much of what we'll say about building ideas involves our fourth assumption and must wait till Part II ("Patterns"), Part I is where we get started. We can't build ideas till we know what their basic units are, which reminds us of our third assumption. Remember we're assuming that all discourse (all complex ideas) can be reduced to a set of basic relations—ways that any two assertions can relate logically to one another.

So Part I—"Relations"—is where we become better acquainted with the ways any two assertions can relate in discourse. To overcome any difficulty we may be having in building complex ideas, the best place to begin is with the simple ideas—relations—that make them up.

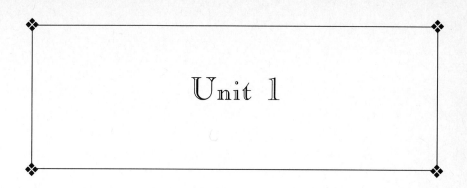

Includer/Included
(Included/Includer)

S omething we all learned as infants, before we had words to help us talk about what we had learned, is that some things include other things. When your mother or father or other caretaker approached your crib several times each day, your infant brain learned to recognize a person, a whole being. But you discovered that the person had a head, a part. And the head included a face, and the face included eyes. In other words, even before you had words to solidify the relationship, you recognized the relationship *whole/part*. The human is a whole, the head a part. And the head can be a whole and the face a part; the face a whole and the eye a part; and the eye a whole and the pupil a part. And on and on, in either direction. This whole/part relationship is one of three we will call *includer/included*, where one term logically includes another term. We will name the three *general/specific*, *whole/part or quality*, and *operation/stage or phase*.

General/Specific (Specific/General)

The *general/specific* relation answers these two questions: "What is *x* a sort of?" and "What is a sort of *x*?" For instance, if I ask you,

"What is an apple a sort of?" one conventional answer would be that an apple is a sort of fruit. So when I ask, "What is *x* a sort of?" I'm asking for a general, an *includer* term for *x*.

apple (specific)/fruit (general)

Fruit includes *apple* (and *peach, plum, apricot,* etc.). When, on the other hand, I ask, "What is a sort of apple?" I'm using *apple* as an includer, a general term, and I'm asking for an included term—for a specific kind or variety of apple.

apples (general)/Golden Delicious, Jonathan, Granny Smith (specific)

The general term is an includer term; the specific term is an included term.

Exercise 1.1

The following are pairs of terms that relate as *general/specific* (or *specific/general*). On a separate sheet of paper, write the numbers of the paired terms and *g/s* if the *general* term is first, *s/g* if the *specific* term is first. If you're unsure of a meaning, use a dictionary.

fly/insect *s/g*   vehicle/car *g/s*
magazine/*Newsweek* *g/s*   Chevrolet/car *s/g*

1. parent/mother
2. vegetable/carrot
3. vegetable/edibles
4. animal/organism
5. animal/dog
6. dog/mammal
7. dog/Saint Bernard
8. dog/bitch
9. house/shelter
10. house/two-story house
11. saxophone/musical instrument
12. weapon/gun
13. pistol/gun
14. pistol/Colt .45
15. pistol/revolver
16. emotion/love
17. Chicago/city
18. source of energy/oil
19. educational institution/college
20. eye/sense organ
21. process/firing ceramics
22. dentistry/profession
23. dentistry/orthodontia
24. dancing/break dancing
25. penal institution/county jail
26. to handle/to wield
27. to transport/to bring
28. putrid/smelly
29. to chastise/to criticize
30. quiet/taciturn

Exercise 1.2

On a separate sheet of paper, pair each of the following terms twice, first with a more general (more inclusive) term, second with a more specific (less inclusive) term. For example, the term *fern* could be coupled with *plant* (a more inclusive term) and with *Boston fern* or *Hawaiian tree fern* (or any other sort of fern), a less inclusive term.

1.	magazine	*6.*	tent
2.	shirt	*7.*	blood
3.	girl	*8.*	anger
4.	alcoholic beverage	*9.*	to fly by jet
5.	rock group	*10.*	election

Whole/Part or Quality (Part or Quality/Whole)

The *general/specific* relation is concerned with kinds, sorts, varieties, types—with the questions "What is *x* a sort of?" and "What is a sort of *x*? The *whole/part* relation answers the questions "What is *x* a part of?" and "What is a part of *x*?"

An apple is a *sort* of fruit. But it might be a *part* of a fruit display or a *part* of an apple tree. Likewise, one *sort* of apple is Golden Delicious. But a *part* of an apple might be the stem or the skin or the core. Another part—a different sort of part—might be the taste or the color or the weight. These "parts" are sometimes called *qualities*, or *components*. The whole/part relation concerns physical structures broken down into substructures and qualities.

Exercise 1.3

The following are pairs of terms that relate as *whole/part* (or *part/whole*). On a separate sheet of paper write the numbers of the paired terms and *w/p* if the *whole* term is first, *p/w* if the *part* term is first. (Remember, *part* can mean quality or component too). Use a dictionary to help you with unfamiliar terms.

Examples: bird/wing   *w/p*   car/used-car lot   *p/w*
  wing/wing feathers   *w/p*   fender/car   *p/w*

1.	doorknob/door	*6.*	eye/iris
2.	house/door	*7.*	iris/blue color
3.	engine/piston	*8.*	library/campus
4.	person/head	*9.*	Kurt/Kurt's
5.	head/eye		left hand

10. Kurt/Kurt's left-handedness
11. heat/summer day
12. pages/textbook
13. December/calendar
14. elasticity/rubber band
15. cake/top layer
16. flour/cake
17. universe/Milky Way galaxy
18. Milky Way galaxy/solar system
19. Mars/solar system
20. cold/ice cube
21. H_2O/H_2
22. virga/cloud

Exercise 1.4

On a separate piece of paper, pair each of the following terms twice, first with a more inclusive (whole) term, second with a less inclusive (part) term. For example the term *fern* could be coupled with *rain forest* (a more inclusive—whole—term) or *frond* (a less inclusive—part—term). Remember that the part may be a structural part or a quality. Use a dictionary for unfamiliar terms.

1. scissors
2. brick
3. guitar
4. platoon
5. pimple
6. campus
7. Exercise 1.4
8. U.S. House of Representatives
9. chromosome
10. electric motor

Operation/Stage or Phase (Stage or Phase/Operation)

The relation *apple/Golden Delicious* is a *general/specific* relation. The Golden Delicious is a specific sort of apple. The relation *apple/stem* is a whole/part relation, the stem being part of an apple. The relation *apple/apple blossom* is what we'll call *operation/stage*. If we think of the word *apple* as applying to the fruit from the time, say, that the flower bud begins to swell in the spring till the ripened fruit drops from the tree in the fall, then *apple* is the name of a process, or an operation, and *apple blossom* is an early stage of that operation. In the relation *operation/stage* the dimension of *time* is involved, and we are dealing with a structure changing in time and space. We're answering the questions "What is *x* a stage of?" and "What is a stage of *x?*"

Exercise 1.5

The following are pairs of terms that relate as *operation/stage* (or *stage/operation*). On a separate piece of paper write the numbers of the paired terms and the letters *o/s* if the *operation* term (the *includer* term) is first, *s/o* if the *stage* term (the *included* term) is first.

  1. inhaling/breathing
  2. running/flexing the right leg
  3. driving to the store/starting the car
  4. painting the trim/painting the house
  5. painting the trim/painting the front-door trim
  6. reading Part I/reading this text
  7. reading Part I/reading Exercise 1.5
  8. getting ready for school/Monday
  9. getting ready for school/getting dressed
  10. getting dressed/finding underwear
  11. finding underwear/opening dresser
  12. talking/moving the tongue
  13. putting polish on cloth/polishing silver
  14. baseball game/fifth inning
  15. top half of fifth/fifth inning
  16. top half of fifth/second out
  17. second out/first batter
  18. first pitch/first batter
  19. lathering shoulders/taking shower
  20. systolic pressure/blood pressure

We should recognize that the name *stage* is sometimes used to refer to two different included units. Just as in the whole/part relationship *part* describes both a physical part (such as "Kurt's left hand") and a quality or characteristic (such as "Kurt's left-handedness"), so the term *stage* applies to an included unit that lasts only until the next stage begins and also to an included unit that lasts indefinitely, sometimes for all of an operation. This second sort of included unit is sometimes called a *phase*.

For example, in the process of an apple's growth, the blossom stage ends when the blossom is pollinated and the fruit-development stage begins. Those are what we'll learn to call coordinate stages; one ends as its coordinate begins. But in the apple's growth process, the nutrient phase goes on from before the blossom opens till the apple drops from the tree. It is still included by the operation term *apple*, but it is a phase, a sort of suboperation, that goes on through the entire operation, as long as nutrients are reaching the developing blossom and fruit.

Exercise 1.6

Following are five pairs of relationships. In each pair, one relationship is operation/stage, the other operation/phase. On a separate sheet of paper, number the paired relationships and label them *o/s* for *operation/stage*, *o/p* for *operation/phase*. Use a dictionary for the terms that don't make sense to you.

> *1. a.* tennis match/first set
>   *b.* tennis match/Hana Mandlikova's activities
> *2. a.* making a dress/handling the material
>   *b.* making a dress/cutting out the material
> *3. a.* mowing the lawn/mowing the side yard
>   *b.* mowing the lawn/pushing the lawnmower
> *4. a.* bird-watching/using your eyes
>   *b.* bird-watching/driving to the estuary
> *5. a.* lifetime/minority
>   *b.* lifetime/metabolism

Exercise 1.7

Ten terms appear in the following list. On a separate piece of paper, pair each term twice—first with a more inclusive (operation) term, second with a less inclusive (stage or phase) term. For example, the term *movie* could be paired with the (more inclusive) operation term *Saturday night date* (where the movie was a *stage* of the evening's activities) and with the (less inclusive) stage term *credits* or *car chase*.

> *1.* school day   *6.* autumn day
> *2.* breakfast   *7.* Hiroshima, 6 August 1945
> *3.* making ice cream   *8.* fueling your car
> *4.* first day on the job   *9.* registering to vote
> *5.* shopping for shoes   *10.* activities of Martin Luther King, Jr.,
>   in Birmingham, Alabama

These, then, are three ways of relating *includer/included* terms: *general/specific* ("What is *x* a sort of?" and "What is a sort of *x*?"); *whole/part* ("What is *x* a part of?" and "What is a part of *x*?"); and *operation/stage, phase* ("What is *x* a stage or phase of?" and "What is a stage or phase of *x*?"). It's not always easy to tell them apart. In fact, it's not *always* necessary to tell them apart. Simply think of these as three basic ways of making large units of small units and small units of large ones.

Exercise 1.8

The following are pairs of assertions that relate as includer/included. Following each pair is a single assertion and a blank. On a separate sheet of paper, write out the assertions. Determine which includer/included relation governs the pair of assertions (general/specific, whole/part, operation/stage). Then, using that same relation, make up an assertion of your own to pair with the single assertion.

Example: Serena sat at the desk. Her face was pale.
A car pulled up. _____

The relation between the first two assertions seems to be whole/part. The picture of Serena sitting at the desk is the whole. The description of her fact concentrates on a part of that whole. What assertion could we add to "A car pulled up" that would concentrate on a part of that whole picture? How about one of these?

Its front fender was crumpled.
Its black paint glistened in the sun.
The headlights were on.
A long crack ran along the bottom of the windshield.

1. A car pulled up. The car was a Ford.
   I'm reading a book. _____
2. The car was a Ford. The car was a 1977 Galaxie.
   He had something wrong with his arm. _____
3. She worked on her motocycle. She changed the headlight.
   He fixed dinner. _____
4. A file cabinet stood in one corner. The bottom drawer was open.
   They looked at the new carpet. _____
5. They were playing a game. They were playing a card game.
   They were playing a card game. _____
6. Jerry was sitting in a chair. His legs were crossed.
   Sylvia stood by the window. _____
7. She cleaned the fish. She slit the belly with a sharp knife.
   He prepared the flower bed. _____
8. We had one problem. We couldn't get a hold of a car.
   My children want a pet. _____
9. Two Holstein cows were lying under a tree. The tree was loaded with tiny red fruit.
   They pulled up in front of an old house. _____
10. Sea gulls circled in the wake of the boat. They screeched shrilly.
    Children raced across the schoolyard. _____
11. She offered them something to eat. She offered them tuna sandwiches.
    She went out to do the chores. _____
12. We heard a strange sound. It was the sound of metal scraping on metal.
    There was one piece of tragic news. _____

Exercise 1.9

The assertions that follow are to be rewritten twice, first with a *more* inclusive term substituted for the underlined term, second with a *less* inclusive term substituted for the underlined term. For example, the assertion

The *hospital* was almost completed

could be written with a more inclusive term this way:

The building was almost completed.

And it could be written with a less inclusive (more specific) term this way:

The ten-story, eighteen-million-dollar Gleason Memorial Hospital was almost completed.

(Notice that your "term" may have several words.)

1. They were having *a soft drink*.
2. His *arm* was broken.
3. His arm was *broken*.
4. She *ran* across the field.
5. She ran across *the field*.
6. I need *new shoes*.
7. The *football game* went into overtime.
8. I could hear *music*.
9. He took *a dime* from the table.
10. *He* took a dime from the table.

Includer/Included Discourse Functions

One way to divide the includer/included relation is according to the sort of analysis being performed. Are we classifying? (that's the general/specific sort); are we analyzing a structure? (that's the whole/part sort); are we breaking a complex event into stages? (that's the operation/stage sort). These are the sorts of division of the includer/included relation we've just done.

Another way to divide the includer/included relation is according to what we might call the *discourse function* we're using it for in our speaking or writing. We'll look here at four discourse functions: *x for example y*, *x particularly y*, *x namely y*, and *x including y*.

x for example y

One of the commonest functions of an *included* element is to provide an example, a typical instance, of an *includer* element. Consider the following *x for example y* units.

1. I hate those TV giveaway shows, like "Let's Make a Deal."
2. Terry asks mature questions for a three-year-old. Just this

morning, for instance, he asked his mom about the government's deficit spending.

3. If we're going to get along as roommates, I'd like for you to change some of your ways. For example, I'd like for you to quit opening my mail.

4. Animals other than man solve problems almost entirely by trial and error rather than by insight. A monkey trapped in a latched box doesn't lie down and ponder what it is he must do to get out. Rather, he starts pawing at various parts of the box, jumping against the sides and the lid, chewing at whatever he can get his mouth on, and so on until he finally trips the latch and escapes.

You'll notice that the *x for example y* relation isn't always signalled by *for example*. Other typical signals include *for instance, such as, like,* and *e.g.* (Latin for *exempli gratia*, which translates "for example"). And sometimes, as in number 4, the relation won't be signalled at all, except by the meaning. In example 4, the first sentence is a generalized statement, the second and third sentences a specific illustration of that generalization. But however it is signalled, the *x for example y* relation is the one we use when our purpose is to give in the *included* assertion a typical example of the *includer* assertion.

Exercise 1.10

On a separate sheet of paper, write out each numbered sentence. Using the relation *x for example y*, generate a second assertion to go with each one. Choose such signal words as *such as, for example, for instance,* and *e.g.* to connect your two assertions. Where a blank appears in the given assertion, provide your own includer term.

Example: I'd like some changes in the _____
I'd like some changes in the house plans. For example, I'd like the upstairs bedroom to be larger.

1. We might do something to make her feel more welcome.
2. Certain things he said made me uneasy.
3. They played several of their most popular numbers.
4. I'd like some changes in _____.
5. A few _____ stand in our way.
6. We bought _____ for the trip.

particularly y

Sometimes the function is to provide not a typical example of the *includer* assertion but a *special* example—the most important example, the best, or whatever. Consider the following *x particularly y* units.

1. They seemed to like the entire meal, especially the fresh asparagus.
2. Fern's children—little Jerry in particular—need more attention and affection.
3. We had a terrific year in sports, particularly in women's volleyball.
4. You shouldn't throw darts at Uncle Ferd's armchair. Certainly, you shouldn't throw darts at Uncle Ferd's armchair when Uncle Ferd is sitting on it.

Typical signals for *x particularly y* include *particularly, especially, primarily, in particular, certainly, foremost, most of all, not the least of all,* and *most important.* When *x particularly y* is made negative, a common signal is *least of all*: "I ain't afraid of nobody, least of all you."

Exercise 1.11

On a separate sheet of paper write out each sentence numbered below. Then, using the relation *x particularly y*, generate a second assertion to pair with each one. Choose signal words such as *particularly, especially, in particular, most of all,* and, when appropriate, *least of all.* Where a blank appears in the given assertion, provide your own includer term.

Example: I like _____.
I like Italian food, especially lasagna.

1. All the students seemed relieved that the test was postponed.
2. She was devastated by the loss of her jewelry.
3. We enjoyed the _____.
4. Wes didn't need trouble that night.
5. Sonja missed the _____.
6. There seems to be some tension between _____.

x namely y

When the function of the *included* term is to exhaust the *includer* term (to provide *all* the examples, parts, or stages), the relation is *x namely y.* This relation is usually not signalled except by punctuation and meaning. But sometimes you'll find the signals *namely* or *specifically* or (very rarely) *viz.* or *to wit.* Consider these *x namely y* examples.

1. We have a problem. We're out of gas.
2. This race will follow the regular course—down Willow Street to Madison; right on Madison to Creole Way; and left on Creole Way to Sanchez Park.
3. Delbert has only one thing going for him: nerve.
4. He brought Laura a box of her favorite candy (Dorothy Pollard's dark chocolate cremes.)

Exercise 1.12

On a separate sheet of paper number the following five assertions and write them out. Then, using the relation *x namely y*, generate an assertion to complete the relation with each assertion provided.

1. She found a real bargain at Macy's.
2. We had forgotten one fact.
3. Two handicaps kept him from qualifying for the job.
4. Do me a favor.
5. Someone had to get the message to Stan.

The *x namely y* relation will often be turned around, so that the *includer* term comes second, as a sort of category term.

He brought Laura a box of Dorothy Pollard's dark chocolate cremes—her favorite candy.

Delbert has nerve, the only thing he has going for him.

Unemployment reached 8.6 percent in November (the highest rate in five years).

Exercise 1.13

The following five assertions are to relate as **reversed** *x namely y* (that is, with the includer term last). On a separate sheet of paper write down the five assertions and complete them with an includer term.

Example: He got an *A* in Algebra.

He got an *A* in Algebra. It was one of three *A*'s he received his freshman year.

1. She and Jonathan were married three weeks later.
2. For breakfast I ate strawberry yogurt.
3. He drives a Datsun.
4. On the table stood a vase filled with red roses.
5. The parakeet was dead.

x including y

The fourth way the *includer/included* relation may function is the relation *x including y*. The main signal words for this relation are *including* and *even*. Again, this relation is often signalled just by punctuation and meaning.

1. Everyone, including Old Man Keyes, showed up for the picnic.
2. He worked every day last week, even Sunday.
3. She sat in front of the TV, her left hand resting on her knee, her right hand poised over the bowl of popcorn.
4. The dry slope was covered with poppies, some of them just starting to bloom.

You'll recall that with *x for example y* the *y* term provides a typical instance of the *x* term. And with *x particularly y* the *y* term provides the most special or true instance of the *x* term. And with *x namely y* the *y* term provides *all* the specifics for the *x* term.

In the *x including y* relation the *y* term is specified for one of two reasons. With the preceding examples 1 and 2, the *y* term specifies information that the audience wouldn't expect to be included in the *x* term. If I say to my audience, "Everyone, even Old Man Keyes, showed up for the picnic," I'm implying that my audience and I find it unusual that Old Man Keyes should have shown up. For whatever reason—because he's a grump or a loner or a man who doesn't like picnics—my audience and I wouldn't expect him at the picnic, and therefore I specify (signalling with *even* or *including*) that he was there.

Another reason an included term is given is simply because the writer or speaker wants you to have that information. The specific information isn't typical, extremely important, or exhaustive. It's just a piece of specific information the writer or speaker wants you to have. Examples 3 and 4 are of this second sort.

Exercise 1.14

On a separate sheet of paper number the following five assertions and write them out. Then, using the *x including y* relation, generate a second assertion for each.

1. Several persons got there early.
2. Don was lying on the bed.
3. My wallet was missing.
4. He served a large platter of fruit.
5. The family owns seven racehorses.

We've spent a great deal of time on the includer/included relations. That's partly because they are so rich and varied. And it's partly because they're so useful in our creating complex ideas. Whenever in our writing or speaking we try to explain something by giving an example or try to make a scene come to life by adding a specific detail, we are using the includer/included relation.

Exercise 1.15

The following are some simple assertions. Expand each one into an includer/included relation by adding your own assertion. Remember the different ways you have to focus your attention:

general/specific

whole/part or quality   and

operation/stage or phase

x for example y

x particularly y

x namely y

x including y

Example: A horse came over the rise.

How might we expand this assertion to an includer/included relation? First, *horse* is more general than, say, *Morgan filly* or *chestnut gelding*. So we could add one of these sentences to make the two relate as general/specific.

A horse came over the rise. It was a Morgan filly.
A horse came over the rise. It was a chestnut gelding.
A horse came over the rise. It was a black-and-white Shetland stallion.
(These reflect the *x namely y* relation)

Or we might consider the horse a *whole* with *parts*.

A horse came over the rise. His mane and tail were matted with burs and caked with mud.
A horse came over the rise. His sleek black hide shone in the slanting sun.
(These reflect the *x including y* relation.)

Or we could recognize that *came over the rise* suggests an operation, an event, and we could concentrate on a stage or phase of that event.

A horse came over the rise. She limped on her right front leg.
A horse came over the rise. She was tossing her head and snorting.
A horse came over the rise. She was pawing and prancing.

And of course nothing keeps us from making "A horse came over the rise" an included element, that is, from adding to the other end.

Just then, animals began appearing from all around us. For example, a horse came over the rise.

Here, then are some assertions for you to add to, to use to make various sorts of includer/included relations. Play with them. Try to discover things the text hasn't mentioned.

1. The children loved the parade.
2. It was an impressive building.
3. The boy ran down the alley.
4. She listened to the sounds in the adjoining room.
5. The car suddenly sped away.
6. I remember my grandmother's house.
7. Then the storm broke.
8. It was my seventh birthday.
9. He looked in the refrigerator for something to eat.
10. They sat on the library steps.
11. He kissed him.
12. He was leaning on the main desk of the library.
13. An announcement was coming over the public-address system.
14. She held a kitten against her shoulder.
15. My father and I were arguing again.

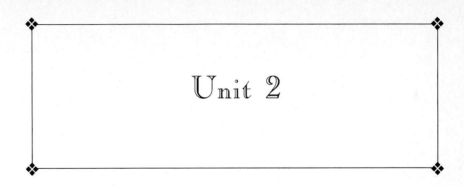

Unit 2

Cause/Effect
(Effect/Cause)

The includer/included relation answers such questions as "What is *x* a sort of?" and "What is a sort of *x*?" The *cause/effect* relation answers such questions as

"What does *x* cause?" and "What causes *x*?"
"What does *x* imply?" and "What implies *x*?"

If you say, "I didn't like that TV program last night," and your roommate asks, "Which TV program?" the relationship suggested is includer/included (for instance *TV program/"Dallas"*). But if you say, "I didn't like that TV program last night," and your roommate asks, "Why not?" the relationship suggested is *cause/effect* (or *effect/ cause*). These two assertions relate as effect/cause:

"I didn't like that TV show last night. There was too much violence."

Exercise 2.1

The numbered units that follow relate as cause/effect or effect/cause. On a separate sheet of paper number the paired units and write *c/e* if the *cause* (or reason) comes first and *e/c* if the *effect* (the result) comes first.

Examples: Steve won't be in this morning. He's at the dentist's office. *e/c*

Since Fred met Eunice, he has been a different guy. *c/e*

1. I can't wear this. It's the wrong color.
2. You did a superb job on my stereo. Now my brother wants you to work on his.
3. Stewart isn't ready yet. He can't find his tennis shoes.
4. A wind came up, sending the dry leaves flying.
5. Whenever E. F. Hutton talks, people listen.
6. I'm losing weight faster. I've been jogging more than usual lately.
7. That sounds horrible! The piano is really out of tune.
8. She beats him regularly at racquetball, so he won't play her anymore.
9. That blistered spot on the coffee table is where Gwen laid her cigarette.
10. The neighbors always call the police when Trudy's lion roars, so Trudy has decided to get rid of it.

Exercise 2.2

The following are single assertions. Use each assertion twice, first as a *cause* for an *effect* assertion you make up, then as an *effect* for a *cause* assertion you make up. For example, the assertion

Carl stormed from the room

could be the cause for this cause/effect relation:

Carl stormed from the room. Everyone seemed uncomfortable.

Or it could be the effect for this cause/effect relation:

Dennis insulted Carl. Carl stormed from the room.

1. Tom gained five pounds last week.
2. The paint is peeling.
3. Many of the pine trees have turned yellow.
4. She took a modeling job.
5. Craig stayed up past midnight.
6. The fullback hasn't gained ten yards yet this afternoon.
7. I have a stomach ache.
8. Now the pages of my magazine are all stuck together.
9. The water warped the kitchen floor.
10. Molly's balloon popped.

One type of cause/effect relation we'll find useful in our discourse—particularly in our persuasive discourse, or argumentation—is what we'll call *evidence/conclusion* (or *conclusion/evidence*). Of course, in our own discourse we won't be drawing conclusions on the basis of *one* piece of evidence. But for now let's just get used to the evidence/conclusion relation, and for that purpose one piece of evidence will serve for one conclusion.

Exercise 2.3

The units that follow relate as evidence/conclusion or conclusion/evidence. Consider the evidence to be the *effect* and the conclusion to be the *reason* or *cause* implied by the evidence. On a separate sheet of paper number the units and write *e/c* if the evidence comes first, *c/e* if the conclusion comes first.

Examples: Sandra's hands are shaking. She must be nervous. *e/c*
The wind is really blowing now. I can see the trees bending and the branches whipping. *c/e*

1. Daryll must really be angry. I've never seen his face so red.
2. The main bearing may be bad. There's oil all over the driveway.
3. The lawn hasn't been mowed in weeks. Maybe they've moved.
4. The tomatoes show black on the tips of the leaves. It must have frosted last night.
5. The dog is barking. Someone may be coming.
6. Look at that eye! You've been in a fight, haven't you?
7. It must be closing time. They just turned off the sign.
8. The radishes need water. They're beginning to wilt.
9. He's not going over too well. The audience is restless.
10. Bonds sales increased. New York City's future looked better.
11. Debbie's not home yet. Maybe that carburetor's acting up again.
12. The band has really been practicing. They executed every maneuver without a mistake.

Exercise 2.4

Ten assertions are given in the following list. Assertions 1 through 5 are *conclusions*. For each of them you are to supply an *evidence* assertion. For example, the *conclusion*

Housing prices have skyrocketed this year

might be coupled with the *evidence*

The Taylors bought a house ten months ago for $90,000 and sold it for $163,500.

Assertions 6 through 10 are *evidence* assertions. For each of them you are to supply a *conclusion* assertion. For example, the *evidence* assertion

Rutledge isn't limping this quarter

might be coupled with this *conclusion*

Rutledge's injury evidently wasn't serious.

1. The baby probably doesn't want any more to eat right now.
2. This knife needs sharpening.
3. Harold is bored.
4. One of your tropical fish seems sick.
5. Somebody must have been here while we were out.
6. There's blood on these Kleenexes in the trash.
7. Agnes is still asleep.
8. Cherries are only thirty-nine cents a pound at three of the local markets.
9. Two of the dogs had cuts on their pads.
10. A brand-new Vega hatchback was parked in the drive.

Some of the formulas we use to indicate the sorts of cause/effect relations treated so far could include *because x, y* (or *x because y*), *x therefore y, x hence y, x so y, x accordingly y,* and *x thus y*. There is another sort of cause/effect relation that we might indicate by the formula *if x, y* or *whenever x, y* or *provided x, y*. Let's call this type *conditional cause/effect*. Under the conditions of *x, y* occurs.

If your tires are underinflated, they wear out faster.
   (conditional cause/effect)
Whenever his wife is out of town, he calls me.
   (conditional cause/effect)
I'll return them, provided that you pay the postage.
   (effect/conditional cause)

And of course this relation can be expressed in *negative* terms too.

Unless he finishes his paper, Mr. Phelps won't accept it.
He has to finish his paper tonight. Otherwise, Mr. Phelps won't accept it.
If he doesn't finish his paper tonight, Mr. Phelps won't accept it.
He has to finish his paper tonight, or else Mr. Phelps won't accept it.

Exercise 2.5

Write ten examples of the *conditional cause/effect* relation, using as many different signals as you can.

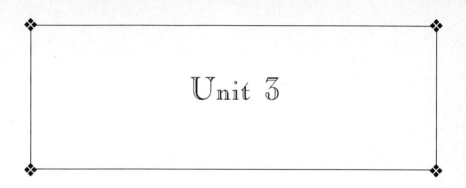

Contrast/Contrast

The *contrast/contrast* relation is concerned with the *difference* between *x* and *y* or the *opposition* of one assertion to another. Some of the formulas suggesting contrast/contrast are *although x, y, true x yet y, x however y, x but y, x on the other hand y, not x rather y,* and *not x instead y*.

1. They didn't do their homework. Instead, they took in a movie.
2. Though Donna was deeply disappointed, she remained composed.
3. We came as boys. We left as men.
4. Sam is six feet five inches tall. Steve is five feet six inches tall.
5. I came to bury Caesar, not to praise him.
6. These aren't pecans; they're almonds.
7. I ordered the bacon-and-tomato sandwich; this is tuna fish.
8. She's eighty-three years old, but she still tends a half-acre garden by herself.
9. Last year he was on academic probation. This year he made the dean's list.
10. It's true that you've never had an accident. But we still have to charge you $663.75 for automobile insurance.
11. Though he searched his entire room, he couldn't find his jogging shoes.
12. Even if both parties agree to negotiate, chances of a settlement look slim.

A contrast/contrast relation that we'll find especially useful in persuasive discourse—discourse used to persuade someone to your point of view—is one we'll call *concession/response* (or *concession/assertion*), represented by the formula *true x yet y*. The cause/effect relation stresses that *y* happens *because of x*. The *concession/response* relation stresses that *y* happens *despite x*. This relation is useful in persuasive writing because it allows you to make your point *in spite of* contrary evidence. In other words, you can use this relation to present your opponent's argument—even to grant the truth of your opponent's argument—and to answer that argument with your own.

It's true that inflation has hit the low-income groups hard. Still, they are financially better off today than they were ten years ago.

Exercise 3.1

The single assertions that follow are to be used twice each, first as the *cause* in a cause/effect relation, then as the *concession* (the *true x* unit) in a concession/assertion relation (*true x yet y*). For example, the assertion

Coffee prices are too high

might be used in this cause/effect relation:

Coffee prices are too high, so I've quit drinking coffee.

Or it might be used in this concession/assertion relation:

Coffee prices are too high, but I've got to have my coffee.

Thus, you will be using the same assertion in an *x therefore y* relation and in a *true x yet y* relation.

1. He had terrible stomach cramps.
2. Your work has been excellent.
3. It's a bad stretch of road.
4. Her family can't afford to put her through college.
5. This was his first roofing job.
6. She's a very demanding teacher.
7. Brian is terrified of snakes.
8. My grandmother is nearly blind.
9. The library reading room was noisy.
10. The rebels had captured the airport.

Another contrast/contrast relation we'll find useful in our writing is one we'll call *positive/negative* (or *negative/positive*), represented by the formula *not x rather y*. There are all sorts of ways to use this relation, a few of which are illustrated as follows without comment.

> She didn't want a Chevy. She wanted a Porsche.
> I come to bury Caesar, not to praise him.
> When I was eighteen I could do two one-handed push-ups; now
>   I can't even do one two-handed push-up.
> He's not a coward. He's very brave.

Quite often the assertions being contrasted are nearly opposite. But sometimes they are just barely distinct from one another. Such very narrow contrasts are useful when we're trying to define precisely. For example, in certain contexts the following pairs of words might be synonyms, that is, each pair of words might mean almost the same thing:

> informal/careless
> plain/flat
> lively/jazzy

But here is how William Watt used them as positive/negative pairs to define what he means by "appropriate for most occasions today":

> I have frankly slanted the book toward the kind of good writing that is appropriate for most occasions today: informal but not careless, plain but not flat, lively but not jazzy.*

Exercise 3.2

The following are twelve words one might use to describe a person or his or her actions. Use each one twice in a *not x rather y* relation, first in the negative (*not x*) assertion then in the positive (*rather y*) assertion. Each time try to choose a term *close to* the meaning of the term listed. For example, the word *upset* might be used in the *not x* assertion this way:

> He wasn't upset. He was just preoccupied.

and this way in the *rather y* assertion:

> He wasn't angry; he was just upset.

Use your dictionary to help you choose terms with only slightly different meanings.

An American Rhetoric, p. viii.

1. nervous
2. tired
3. cute
4. inquisitive
5. solemn
6. pugnacious
7. repulsive
8. amused
9. generous
10. devious
11. reserved
12. lenient

Exercise 3.3

Write ten pairs of assertions relating as contrast/contrast, either *not x rather y* or *true x yet y*.

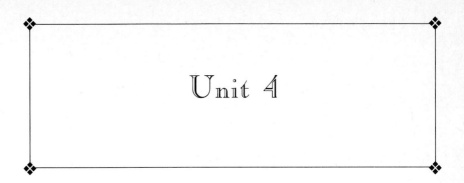

Comparison/Comparison

The contrast/contrast relation is concerned with the difference between *x* and *y*, with how two assertions are opposed; the *comparison/comparison* relation is concerned with similarity, with how two assertions are alike. Comparison/comparison answers the question "How are *x* and *y* alike?" Formulas suggesting comparison/comparison include *x like y, just as x so y, x as if y, x the way y, x in the same way y, x similarly y,* and *x likewise y.*

1. She treats him like a dog.
2. She smiled and looked down, the way her father used to.
3. He danced clumsily, as if he were wearing swim fins.
4. They screamed like banshees.
5. Just as I wouldn't choose a hungry fox to guard my henhouse, so I wouldn't elect Howard treasurer right after the courts raised his ex-wife's alimony payment.

Exercise 4.1

Following are five assertions. Expand them by using the *comparison/comparison* relation. For example, the assertion

He entered the room self-consciously

might be expanded this way:

He entered the room self-consciously, like a six-year-old walking in on attentive adults.

1. It smelled musty.
2. He bolted the sandwich down in two bites.
3. A light flickered briefly on the horizon.
4. The ducks floated motionlessly on the still pond.
5. She drew back from him quickly.

Exercise 4.2

One of the tendencies of new writers is to grab the first comparison that comes to their minds. The problem is that the first comparison that comes to their minds has probably been used before, many times. Such timeworn comparisons are called clichés. Good writers avoid clichés ("like the plague," a less good writer might say). Following are the frames for eight comparisons. Write down the first comparison that comes to mind (it will be a cliché, assuming that you have been paying attention to what people usually say). Then write down another comparison—a fresh one.

1. mad as a . . .
2. sly as a . . .
3. slippery as an . . .
4. quick as a . . .
5. solid as a . . .
6. quiet as a . . .
7. happy as a . . .
8. bitter as . . .

Exercise 4.3

Write out ten comparison/comparison relations of your own, using such formulas as *x like y, x in the same way y, just as x so y, x likewise y,* and *x similarly y.*

Exercise 4.4

Sometimes comparion/comparison will be negative rather than positive. Probably the most common formula for negative comparison/comparison is *no more x than y*:

He could no more beat Sue at tennis than I could beat Bobby Fisher at chess.

Try four sentences of your own using the *no more x than y* formula.

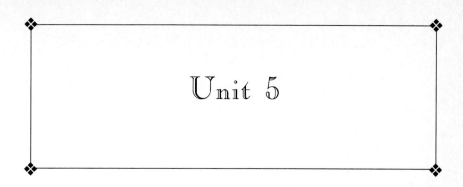

Unit 5

Assertion/Intensification; Assertion/Regression

These two relations answer the questions "Can I go farther?" and "Have I gone too far?"

First, let's assume that you haven't eaten for sixty hours and that you say

"I'm hungry."

Then you decide that you can really go farther than that. You're not merely hungry; you're famished. The relation between the assertions "I'm hungry" and "I'm famished" (assuming that's the order we deliver them in) is the relation *assertion/intensification:*

"I'm hungry. In fact, I'm famished."

The second assertion is stronger than the first, more intense. That's why we're calling it *assertion/intensification.* Here are a few more examples, using other signal words.

He was tired, indeed, exhausted.
Jane was decent last night, even pleasant.

It was a warm evening, almost hot.
Jerry's estimate was high—perhaps too high.

Now let's assume that instead of understating the case (stating that you're hungry when in fact you've never been so hungry in your life), you've overstated the case. You've said

"I'm famished"

when in fact you were merely ready to eat a little something. "I'm famished" is too intense. After you've said it, you decide to back off a bit, to *regress:*

"I'm famished. Well, at least I'm hungry."

Assertion/regression is characterized by just such backing off, such regressing. Here are a few more examples.

This car has been giving me trouble all week—since Wednesday anyway.
It's too expensive. At any rate, I can't afford it.
He'll be here later. Well, he said he would be.
Hildegard's dog is dead. At least he hasn't moved since that truck hit him three days ago.

Exercise 5.1

The following are ten assertions that you are to use as the first unit in assertion/intensification. The positive signals you'll find most useful include *in fact, for that matter, indeed, if not,* and *even.* The assertion "Sam was tired" might be intensified this way: "Sam was tired. In fact he was exhausted." Or "Sam was tired, if not exhausted." The most common negative signal is *not x let alone y,* as in "He never pays for his own dinner, let alone treats me."

1. Brunhilda is fat.
2. Dallas is the nicest city in Texas.
3. He couldn't remember my name.
4. Larry likes dogs.
5. Professor Jenkins was angry.
6. It was a bumpy plane ride.
7. We could hear people arguing.
8. That was the hardest test I ever took.
9. Downhill skiing is a dangerous sport.
10. John never phones his parents.

Exercise 5.2

The same ten assertions can also be expanded by the assertion/regression relation. In the previous exercise (5.1) you might have expanded "Brunhilda is fat" this way:

Brunhilda is fat. In fact, she's downright obese.

Or this way:

Brunhilda is fat. Indeed, her whole family is fat.

This time you will be expanding not by intensification but by regression. So the signals you'll find most useful are *at least, anyway, at any rate,* and *well.*

Brunhilda is fat. Well *I* think she's fat, anyway.

Or

Brunhilda is fat, or at least overweight.

Expand the remaining nine assertions of Exercise 5.1 by assertion/regression.

Exercise 5.3

Try expanding the following assertions by intensifying first one part of the assertion then another. For example, the assertion

John forgot my birthday this year

could be intensified first by focusing on *John:*

John forgot my birthday this year. In fact even my parents forgot my birthday this year.

Then it could be intensified by focusing on *this year:*

John forgot my birthday this year, and last year too, for that matter.

Thus, for each of the five assertions that follow you will write two assertion/intensification relations, focusing first on one part, then on another.

1. Joe made some negative remarks about Darlene.
2. Someone mentioned that you and Doug were dating.
3. The lighting for last night's production was rather poor.
4. I don't enjoy soap operas.
5. My computer has been on the blink this week.

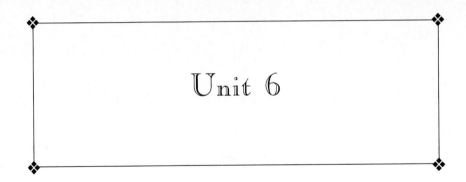

Unit 6

Location/Assertion

The *location/assertion* relation answers such questions as "When does the assertion apply?" or "Where does the assertion apply?" or "Who made this assertion?" The most common uses of this relation are to establish the *time* or the *place* or the *source* that governs an assertion:

In April of 1977 the family bought a grocery store.
On top of every table, desk, shelf, and chair in the room, Jerry had stacked his books.
According to Freud, the relationship between the mother and the infant is the crucial one.

Location/assertion is a very common relation, though perhaps not as common as it seems at first. Often what seems to be establishing the location of an assertion (especially the *time* or *place*) is primarily a cause (in cause/effect) or a contrast (in contrast/contrast). Look at the following three sentences, all beginning with a *where* element. One *where* element is *location*, one is *cause*, and one is *contrast*. Can you see which is which?

1. Where my uncle had parked his car, there was a big pool of fresh oil.
2. Where John once would eat ten or twelve pancakes for breakfast, now he eats two at most.
3. Where my uncle parks his car there is a beautiful catalpa tree in full bloom.

The *where* element in item 1 suggests a *cause* in a cause/effect relation. The implication is that the oil is there because it came from my uncle's car. The *where* element in item 2 relates as contrast/contrast. (Often—indeed usually—we will use *whereas* instead of *where* to signal this relation.) Only in item 3 is the *where* element simply establishing the location, the place, of a location/assertion relation.

Exercise 6.1

Five pairs of sentences appear in the following list. In each pair one sentence is primarily location/assertion, the other primarily cause/effect or contrast/contrast. Determine in each case which is the location/assertion sentence. Determine also whether the remaining sentence is contrast/contrast or cause/effect.

1. *a.* Where he had left the hose running, the new grass had washed away.
   b. Where I work, they always have an office party at Christmas.
2. *a.* When she got up, the sun was shining.
   b. When she got up, the room started spinning.
3. *a.* Where my old house had stood, there is now an apartment building.
   b. In back of my old house there used to be an orchard.
4. *a.* Since I don't have a license, you'll have to drive.
   b. Since late last month no one has seen him.
5. *a.* The day Doug turned twenty-one, Reagan was reelected president.
   b. The day Doug turned twenty-one, his parents told him he simply had to get a job and move out.

Exercise 6.2

The *location* stage of the location/assertion relation establishes *time* (the *when* of the assertion), *place* (the *where*), or what we might call *credentials* (the *according to whom*). For example, the assertion

The desert is beautiful

might be expanded in each of the following three ways:

(time)   In the spring the desert is beautiful.
(place)   In southern Utah the desert is beautiful.
(credentials)   According to Edward Abbey, the desert is beautiful.

Expand each of the following assertions three times using location/assertion: first by time, then by place, then by credentials.

1. They made a very good clam chowder.
2. Greg was afraid of moths.
3. They will be opening a new supermarket.
4. The football team was a real powerhouse.

Exercise 6.3

In the last exercise we expanded assertions by adding a location stage—of time, place, or credentials. For example, we expanded

The desert is beautiful

with the units *in the spring, in southern Utah,* and *according to Edward Abbey* to make three new sentences. Of course, all three units could be added in one sentence, for instance

According to Edward Abbey, the desert in southern Utah is beautiful in the spring.

Or perhaps

The southern Utah desert in spring is beautiful, according to Edward Abbey.

In this exercise see if you can make a single sentence out of each of the sets of three sentences you wrote for Exercise 6.2. Make what changes you need to.

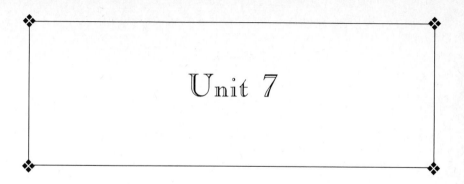

Manner/Assertion;
Evaluation/Assertion

M*anner/assertion* answers the question "In what way or manner did it happen?" *Evaluation/assertion* answers the question "What is the speaker or writer's feeling or attitude toward what happened?" A quick illustration will help show how these two differ and why they are treated together. In the sentence

Jorge looked unhappily at Maria

the word *unhappily* expresses the manner, the way, in which Jorge looked at Maria. The sentence says that Jorge looked at Maria in an unhappy fashion. The relation here is *manner/assertion*. But in the sentence

Unhappily, the pool won't be finished until fall

the word *unhappily* expresses how the writer feels about the fact that the pool won't be finished until fall. In other words, *unhappily* doesn't express the way or manner the pool won't be finished; rather, it expresses the writer's evaluation of the *fact* that the pool won't be finished until fall:

> The pool won't be finished until fall; I consider that an unhappy situation.

This relation is *evaluation/assertion*.

Exercise 7.1

A list of five pairs of sentences follows. In each pair, one sentence expresses an evaluation/assertion (or assertion/evaluation) relation; the other expresses a manner/assertion (or assertion/manner) relation. Be able to identify each.

1. *a.* Strangely enough, Jeanne didn't come home.
   b. Jeanne looked strangely at Martha.
2. *a.* She smiled ironically at me.
   b. Ironically, she smiled at me.
3. *a.* He looked remarkably like his father.
   b. He looked, remarkably, like his father.
4. *a.* They spoke hopefully about returning to their village.
   b. Hopefully, they'll be able to return to their village.
5. *a.* I find, regrettably, that I've lost your wallet.
   b. Mark stared into his empty glass regretfully.

Exercise 7.2

Write five pairs of sentences (as in Exercise 7.1) in which the same word or similar words will signal *manner* the first time and *evaluation* the second.

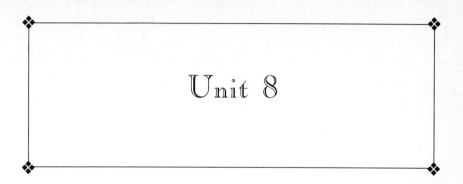

Coordinate/Coordinate [/Coordinate]

This last relationship we'll treat differs from all the other relationships in two ways:

First, all the other relationships have only two elements, two chunks: cause/effect, includer/included, assertion/intensification, and so on. The *coordinate/coordinate* relationship likewise can have two elements. But it can also have three or four or nine or sixteen or a thousand. In other words, while signal words such as *but* or *so* or *in fact* can connect only two chunks of information, signal words like *and*, *or*, and *nor* can connect any plural number; three or more coordinate chunks will be called a *series*.

Second, all the other relations are what we can call "self-defined." We know *x* is a cause because *y* is its effect. And we know *y* is the effect because we regard *x* as its cause. But the coordinate/coordinate relationship is what we can call "other defined"—*x* and *y* are coordinate not primarily because of the relation they bear to one another; rather it is because they bear the same relation to another element, another chunk. That is to say we consider two chunks coordinate because they are both effects of the same cause, or causes of the same effect, or parts of the same whole, or stages of the same operation, or whatever.

We'll look more closely at these two principles later, especially in Part II. For now, let's look at five expressions of the coordinate/coordinate relationship: *x and y [and z]*, *x or y [or z]*, *x that is y [that is z]*, *neither x nor y [nor z]*, and *x and/or y [and/or z]*.

The first two of these five relations can be considered basic; the other three are derived from these two.

x and y [and z]

When we simply *add* elements in pairs or in a series, we're using the coordinate relationship *x and y [and z]*. Five examples of this relationship appear in the following list. Note that signal words other than *and** may be used and that sometimes no signal word at all is used.

1. The inner planets are Mercury, Venus, Earth, and Mars.
2. She will be swimming two kilometers plus bicycling fifty kilometers plus running twenty kilometers.
3. The housing project was built on an old toxic-waste dump site. Moreover, an earthquake fault runs within a hundred yards of the project. In addition, the project is located downstream from an earth-fill dam cited as unsafe in a recent geologic survey.
4. They filled and stacked sandbags. They added two feet of earth to the levees. They drained thousands of gallons of water from the reservoirs. Then they waited.
5. He brought a bottle of wine. She brought three kinds of cheese.

x or y [or z]

The second basic coordinate/coordinate relationship is *x or y [or z]*. The best way to see the difference between this and the previous relation is to do a little basic math. If I say to you,

"Bring a salad, a main dish, and a dessert,"

how many things am I asking you to bring? Obviously, I'm asking you to bring three things. But if I say to you,

---

*And is sometimes used to signal relationships other than coordinate/coordinate also—for example cause/effect ("She smiled, and he smiled back") and conditional cause/effect ("Do that again and I'm leaving.")

"Bring a salad, a main dish, *or* a dessert,"

how many things am I asking you to bring? Just one.

Or joins three *chunks* of information, just as *and* did. The difference is that with *and* you add up the three chunks, while with *or* you choose one of them—any alternative, but just one.

Following are five examples of this relationship. While *or* and *either . . . or* are by far the most common signals, certain other signals are also used, including *as an alternative, alternatively,* and *on the other hand* (though these signals almost always join just two chunks). Occasionally (as in item 5 of the list that follows), the relationship is signalled by an outside sentence (context).

1. We need a cable, a chain, or a heavy rope.
2. The dinner comes with soup, salad, fruit cup, or a slice of melon.
3. He may be badly hurt. On the other hand, he may be faking again.
4. Larry's either a Latter-day Saint or a Seventh-Day Adventist.
5. You may stay here by yourself. You may go with us. It's up to you.

x that is to say y [that is to say z]

The signal *or* is used for two different relations. We just looked at one—one that offers a choice between two different things. In example 4 in the preceding list—

Larry's either a Latter-day Saint or a Seventh-Day Adventist

—we've offered the name of two different religious groups and said that Larry is a member of one or the other, not both. But there is another way *or* can offer a choice, as in this sentence:

Sonja is a Latter-day Saint, or a Mormon.

To see the essential difference between this sentence and example 4 from the preceding list, you need to know these facts: Latter-day Saints and Seventh-Day Adventists are two different religious groups; Latter-day Saints and Mormons are two different *names* for the *same* religious group.

Before we go on, notice one additional difference between the two sentences: one of them has a comma before the *or;* the other one doesn't. In fact, it is the comma, not the *or*, that tells careful readers that the second sentence offers a choice between two *names* for the same thing, not a choice between two things.

So we'll call the relation that offers a choice between two (or more) *things* the relation *x or y [or z]*. And we'll call the relation that offers a choice between two (or more) *expressions of* the same information *x that is to say y [. . . z]*, or *assertion/reassertion*.

Following are five sentences representing the formula *x that is to say y [that is to say z]*. Notice the signal words, the punctuation, and the meaning relations that tell the reader that the choice is not between two (or more) things but is rather between two (or more) names for the same thing.

1. His father works for the CIA (Central Intelligence Agency).
2. The most common weed pest in the valley is redroot, also called pigweed.
3. I was pooped, bushed, worn out, spent.
4. Your services will no longer be needed by our organization. In other words, you're fired.
5. There is no life without death. Every living creature must ultimately die.

Exercise 8.1

This exercise asks you to distinguish between the relation *x or y* (which offers a choice between two or more different things) and the relation *x that is to say y* (which offers a choice between two or more names for the same thing or expressions of the same meaning). In the following list are ten sentences, representing either relation. On a separate sheet of paper number the sentences and identify the formula for each—*x or y* or *x that is to say y*. Use a dictionary if you need help.

1. I'll have to sell my banjo, my mandolin, or my guitar.
2. Vamoose! Get out! Scram! Exit!
3. We plan to visit Fort Lauderdale or Orlando.
4. We plan to visit Reno, "the biggest little city in the world."
5. Sodium nitrite has been clearly identified as a carcinogen—or cancer-causing agent.
6. The operation is done by laser (light amplification by stimulated emission of radiation).
7. She played racquetball, jogged, swam, or did aerobic dancing each morning.
8. The afternoon was muggy, sultry, humid.
9. He either jumped, fell accidentally, or was pushed.
10. The population was, in the original sense of the word, decimated: one of every ten persons died of the plague.

Exercise 8.2

Students often have difficulty distinguishing between *x that is to say y* and a relation we looked at much earlier: *x namely y*. Certainly they resemble one another, in that the *y* element in each case is a sort of restatement of the *x* unit. But they differ in this: with *x namely y* the *y* unit is a more specific expression of the *x* unit ("He wanted only one thing for Christmas: an amplifier for his guitar"); with *x that is to say y*, on the other hand, the *y* unit and the *x* unit are at the same level of inclusiveness ("He wanted only one thing for Christmas, a single yuletide present").

On a separate sheet of paper, number the sentences and identify the formula for each—*x that is to say y* or *x namely y*.

1. I need a cup of coffee, or "Brazilian bean soup," as my uncle Ralph calls it.
2. There's one thing I need first thing in the morning: a cup of coffee.
3. He brought her a box of chocolates—maple cremes.
4. He brought her a present, a box of chocolates.
5. He brought her a present, a little gift.
6. Dotting the hillside on the other side of the ravine were thirty or forty wapiti, American elk.
7. Dotting the hillside on the other side of the ravine were thirty or forty wapiti (*Cervus canadensis*).
8. I found two things missing: my stereo and my Kermit the Frog telephone.
9. He has halitosis, bad breath.
10. He has a problem, halitosis.

[neither] x nor y [nor z]

If I say, "Bring a salad, a main dish, and a dessert," I'm asking that you bring three items. If I say, "Bring a salad, a main dish, or a dessert," I'm asking that you bring one item (your choice). If I say, "Bring a main dish, an entree," I'm still asking for one item; I'm just giving you two different names for it. These are the three relations we've just looked at: *x and y [and z], x or y [or z],* and *x that is to say y [that is to say z]*.

But how many items am I asking for if I say, "Bring neither a salad, a main dish, nor a dessert"? The answer is *zero*. The relation *[neither] x nor y [nor z]* is one result of applying *negative* to either of our first two relations:

He had a good job, a new car, and a house in the suburbs +
[negative] = He had neither a good job, a new car, nor a house
in the suburbs.

(There is, of course, a perfectly legitimate way to negate using *or:* He didn't have a good job, a new car, or a house in the suburbs.)

The relation *[neither] x nor y [nor z]* offers one special problem: when *nor* connects full assertions (full sentences), we need to change the position of the first word in the second sentence and alter the verb, as in the example that follows:

She had time to shower. And she had time to fix her hair [+ negation] = She didn't have time to shower. Nor did she have time to fix her hair.

Exercise 8.3

Practice the operation just described (we can call it the "*nor* inversion") by rewriting the four pairs of sentences below as *x nor y.* (You might find that one inversion sounds better with *neither* than with *nor.*) Use a separate sheet of paper.

   1. He finished his homework. And he got a full night's sleep. [+ negation]
   2. They will be open today. And they will be open tomorrow. [+ negation]
   3. The Reyeses are going with us next week. And the Smiths are too. [+ negation]
   4. I found my keys. And I found my wallet. [+ negation]

x and/or y [and/or z]

This last coordinate/coordinate relationship is rather uncommon. But you will encounter it in your reading, and you should know how it's used. Remember our number game:

Bring a salad, a main dish, and a dessert.   (3 items)

Bring a salad, a main dish, or a dessert.   (1 item)

Bring an entree, a main dish.   (1 item)

Bring neither a salad, a main dish, nor a dessert.   (0 items)

Our final relation presents the last mathematical possibility:

Bring a salad, a main dish, and/or a dessert.   (1, 2, or 3 items)

Our final relation is a result of *combining* our first two relations.

Exercise 8.4

Examine each of the following sentences, and see if you can explain to your classmates why each presents more than one mathematical possibility:

1. For dessert you may have pie, cake, and/or brownies.
2. We can watch *Monty Python and the Holy Grail* and/or *Jabberwocky* and/or *The Meaning of Life*.

These, then, are the logical relations that make up all the complex ideas you read or write. We have a great deal more to do with combining them—the focus of Part II and Part III. But even before we begin to combine two and three and more relations at a time to make complex ideas, there is a use we may put them to in the service of our writing.

❖————————————————————————❖

Essay Assignment One
Prewriting Exercises:
Brainstorming and Freewriting

When my high school buddy Al took me out on the golf course that day to teach me how to swing a club, the first mistake he made was to tee up four or five balls and drive them out of sight as I watched. Not only was the target he had set out of my sight; it was also beyond my reach.

When we're first learning to write, it's likewise easy to set too distant a goal the first few times or to have too distant goals set for us. I remember being asked in the eighth grade to write a term paper on a subject of my choice. I chose to write on ants. Actually, I chose to copy various paragraphs from several encyclopedia articles on ants. It wasn't a very profitable exercise. It was like playing a round of golf by letting Al swing the club.

These first two writing assignments have a fairly modest target. The target is not a 500-word theme—nor indeed a theme of any length. The target is merely to get you to write for a while, first in a mode sometimes called "brainstorming," then in a mode sometimes called "freewriting."

Brainstorming: Clustering and Chaining Relationships

Brainstorming allows us to explore a subject—to discover ideas we already have on the subject and to discover areas we might want to learn more about. Any activity aimed at this type of discovery can be called brainstorming, but here we'll work with two sorts of brainstorming: clustering and chaining.

Clustering and chaining both explore relationships. With clustering, one element in the relationship remains constant. With chaining, a new element is introduced with each relationship. Let's see how it works.

First, with either clustering or chaining, it's best to have a large area to work—a *large* sheet of paper or a blackboard. Second, we need a subject, a topic.

For the sake of illustration, let's take the painting *Northbound*, depicted on the cover of your text, as the subject. In the middle of your sheet of paper or in the center of the blackboard, write the name and draw a circle around it:

This circle forms half a relation. To form the other half, we need another term, also circled, and a line connecting them that specifies the relation. For example, we might consider *Northbound* a whole and the sea gull one of its parts. We represent the relation this way:

A "cluster" results when the same term forms half of a number of relations, as in the illustration below:

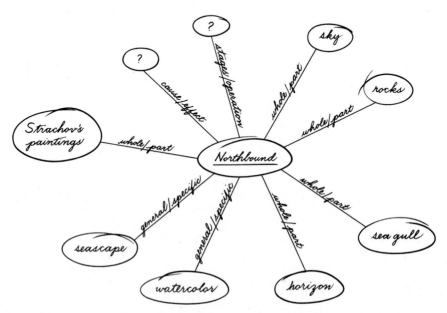

Before we leave clustering to look at chaining, note that two of our circles contain question marks. They denote areas we lack information about, information that we may want to learn. The cause/effect relation might ask, "Was there a special reason (cause) that inspired Gregory Strachov to paint this particular picture?" The stage/operation relation might ask, "What was a particular stage in the process (operation) of painting *Northbound?* These two question-marked circles remind us that one of the functions of brainstorming is to suggest areas where we might be seeking more information.

In clustering we find several relations radiating from a single term. Chaining, by contrast, involves shifting our attention from one term to the next. For example, to return to our first relation—

—if instead of forming another relation with *Northbound* we form another with *sea gull,* we've started a chain:

And we can continue that chain as far as we choose (or at least as far as space allows).

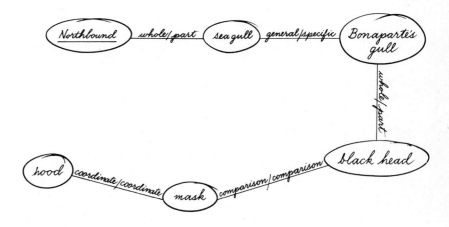

Chaining and clustering can be combined, of course. For example, *black head* can form its own little cluster.

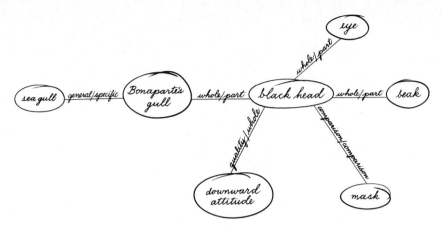

Now that you have the idea, do your own brainstorming. Either continue exploring *Northbound* or explore another topic, whichever your teacher suggests. In either case, try to use *all* the relations treated in Part I.

Freewriting:
Letting the
Ideas Happen

Another way to explore a subject is through what we call freewriting. In freewriting, many things don't count. Spelling doesn't count, nor does sentence structure, nor organization nor development. The only thing that counts is to put on paper whatever you're thinking.

Set yourself a time limit (ten or fifteen minutes should do). Get a couple of sheets of paper and a pen or pencil. Place *Northbound* where you can look at it. Then simply begin to write—whatever comes into your head.

If what comes into your head is, "I don't know why I'm even doing this stupid exercise," write it down. Don't cross words out. Don't sit and think. Just write whatever comes into your mind for the ten or fifteen minutes you've scheduled.

When you've finished, there may well be a sentence or two that suggest an idea worth pursuing. That's the whole purpose of both brainstorming and freewriting—to explore a topic until some worthwhile ideas pop up.

Part II

Patterns

Introduction

In Part I ("Relations") we studied the ways any pair of assertions might relate to one another. We saw, for example, that such assertions as

I'm tired, so I'm going to bed

relate as cause/effect (*x*/*therefore y*), while the assertions

I'm tired, but I'm going to finish my homework

relate as concession/assertion (*true x*/*yet y*). Our task in Part I was to learn the basic ways any two assertions can relate.

In Part II we'll look at the *patterns* we can develop with three or more assertions—look, in other words, at the patterns we call discourse. Discourse is what happens when we put relations together.

To simplify matters in the long run, we are going to use two somewhat artificial devices in Part II. Because these are artificial devices, I need to tell you now that what we produce as discourse in Part II is not what we want finally to produce as discourse. (The differences will be differences in style.) But the activities in Part II are a step we need to take.

One of these artificial devices is this: in Part II we will usually write each assertion in each exercise as an independent (base) clause, or what we'll call a "full assertion." In Part I we illustrated relations with pairs of assertions. Sometimes both assertions were independent clauses (full assertions).

Barry had stomach flu. Therefore, he missed the game.
or
Barry had stomach flu, so he missed the game.

Sometimes only one of the assertions in the pair was independent, the other a dependent element of some sort:

Because he had stomach flu, Barry missed the game.
or
Barry missed the game because he had stomach flu.
or
Suffering from stomach flu, Barry missed the game.
or
Due to his stomach flu Barry missed the game.

In the four preceding sentences "Barry missed the game" is an independent clause; the other elements are dependent elements—modifiers of one sort or another. Both the independent clause and the modifier are *assertions* in each case, but only one of those assertions—the independent clause, or full assertion—could be punctuated by itself as a full sentence.

One of the artificial devices that we will follow in Part II, then, is usually to combine full, independent-clause assertions.

So when we combine assertions in Part II we will get such combinations as

Barry had stomach flu and Chad had a sprained ankle, so they missed the game.

But we usually won't get such combinations as

Because Barry had stomach flu and Chad a sprained ankle, they missed the game.

This is not to say that the second combination is wrong. In fact, it is more sophisticated and mature than the first. It is merely to say that we won't be trying many combinations such as the second one till we get to Part III.

The second artificial device we'll be using in Part II is a type of diagram. The function of the diagram is to show how the assertions relate to one another—to help us sort our assertions into chunks.

The simplest diagrams merely divide two assertions and name their relation:

```
                              and
                               ┬
      ────────────────────────────────────────────────
              coordinate      │      coordinate

         I'd like a bowl of chili │ I'd like a glass of milk
```

But the diagrams get more complex as we add assertions:

```
              namely
               ┬
  ──────────────────────────────────────────────────────────
     includer  │                    included
               │                      and
               │                       ┬
               │           ──────────────────────────────
               │            coordinate │   coordinate

 I'd like something to eat │ I'd like a bowl of chili │ I'd like a glass of milk
```

concession	but includer	namely	included and coordinate	coordinate
I don't have much time	I'd like something to eat		I'd like a salad	I'd like a cup of tea

concession	but		assertion		
	includer	namely included			
		coordinate	or	coordinate	
		and coordinate	coordinate	and coordinate	coordinate
I don't have much time	I'd like something to eat	I'd like a bowl of chili	I'd like a glass of milk	I'd like a salad	I'd like a cup of tea

Of course, the diagrams can soon get cumbersome. And if we continued to print the assertions right in the diagrams, they would get cumbersome even sooner. So in Part II we will print the assertions and the diagrams separately, and we will code the letters into the diagrams to show the chunking—the relationships among the assertions.

Usually, instead of using terms such as "coordinate/coordinate" or "includer/included," we'll represent the relationship by a simple code of two letters and a *signal word* or two: *x and y, x namely y, if x, y, not x rather y, x in fact y.*

For the moment, let's get some practice using these diagrams. Following are four sets of three assertions each. Each set is accompanied by a diagram and the names of the two relations involved in that set. Your task will be to put the names of the relations on the proper levels in the diagram. For example, look at the following set:

a. I'm hungry
b. I'm starving
c. Let's get something to eat
● (*x so y, x in fact y*)

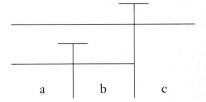

If we read *a*, *b*, and *c* in order, as a single piece of discourse, we recognize that *a* and *b* relate as *x, in fact y*, or as assertion/intensification. And we recognize that the *set ab* (the two assertions together) relate as a *cause* for *c* (the *effect*). So we could fill in the diagram this way:

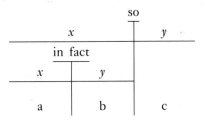

Now try copying and completing these four diagrams. Be prepared to discuss your decisions. Also, be prepared to discuss other chunking patterns each set of assertions might take.

1. a. I've finished my
   homework
   b. I've finished reading
   two chapters of history
   c. I've finished writing
   my report for psychol-
   ogy
   ● (*x namely y, x and y*)

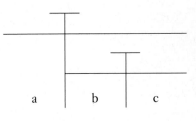

2. *a.* The car was badly
     damaged
   b. The whole front end
     was crushed in
   c. No one was injured
   ● (*x but y, x namely y*)

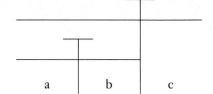

a   b   c

3. *a.* We won our division
   b. I'm going to celebrate
     tonight
   c. I may celebrate
     through tomorrow
   ● (*x in fact y, x so y*)

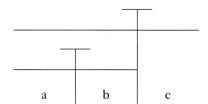

a   b   c

4. *a.* We need several
     things from the store
   b. We need bread
   c. Nothing is open at this
     hour
   ● (*x particularly y, x but y*)

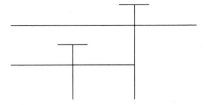

a   b   c

Now let's try four more sets, a little more challenging. This time the assertions *may not be in logical order.* So your task will first be to put them in logical order (by coding their letters into the diagram) and will then be to fill in the diagram with the proper relations. Let's try this practice set first:

a. It's raining
b. We'd better move the party
   indoors
c. The wind is blowing
● (*x and y, x so y*)

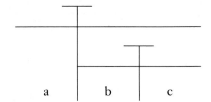

It's fairly obvious that "it's raining" and "the wind is blow-ing" are coordinate/coordinate and that *together* they constitute the *cause* for moving the party indoors. So we might fill in our diagram this way:

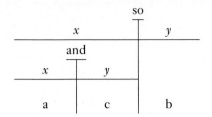

"It's raining and the wind is blowing, so we'd better move the party indoors."

But note that *a* and *c* are the sort of coordination that is reversible, so we could also fill in our diagram this way:

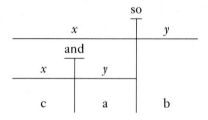

"The wind is blowing and it's raining, so we'd better move the party indoors."

Here, then, are four sets to do on your own. Play with these sets, discovering what you can about the patterns.

1. *a.* She bought some bait
   b. She bought some fish-hooks
   c. She bought some things for the fishing trip
   ● (*x namely y, x and y*)

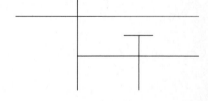

2. *a.* She bought some bait
   b. She forgot the fish-hooks
   c. She bought two dozen nightcrawlers
   ● (*x namely y, x but y*)

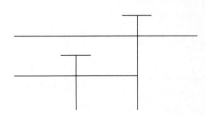

3. *a.* She bought some bait
   b. She bought a jar of salmon eggs
   c. She bought two dozen nightcrawlers
   ● (*x and y, x including y*)

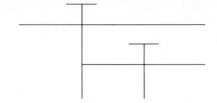

4. *a.* She drove to the sporting goods store
   b. She bought two dozen nightcrawlers
   c. She bought bait for the fishing trip
   ● (*x and y, x including y*)

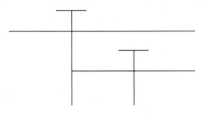

One more set of four and we're ready to try some exercises. This time the diagram has already been filled in, so we know what the relations are. What is missing is one of the three assertions. So this time you are asked to generate an assertion that would fit logically with the other two in the diagram.

Again, an illustration or two should help:

1. *a.* The chair had a broken spindle
   b. The chair was damaged
   c. _____

What we need to fill in the blank is another way the chair was damaged—a coordinate assertion to "the chair had a broken spindle." Here are three possible assertions for *c*: "The chair had a deep scratch on the back"; "The cane seat was badly torn"; "One of the legs was missing."

Now, here's a different chunking pattern:

2. *a.* The chair had a broken spindle
   b. The chair was damaged
   c. _____

```
                        and
            x            |            y
         _____
              namely
         x        |        y
       _____

         b        |        a              c
```

This time our missing assertion coordinates with the *set ba*; that is, this time we're looking for an assertion coordinate with "the chair was damaged." Again, here are three possible assertions for *c*: "The table was also damaged"; or "The chair didn't match our decor"; or "The chair was overpriced." Now, copy and complete the four diagrams below. Be prepared to discuss your decisions. Also be prepared to discuss other chunking patterns each set of assertions might take.

1. a. He had a deep bruise under his right eye
   b. His face was a mess
   c. _____

```
              namely
         x      |        y
       _____
                        and
                   x      |      y
                 _____

         b              a            c
```

2. a. Donna lost her keys
   b. Her keys included the one to her locker
   c. _____

```
            including
         x      |        y
       _____
                        and
                   x      |      y
                 _____

         a              b            c
```

3. a. I could break my date
   b. I could do one of two things
   c. _____

```
              namely
         x      |        y
       _____
                         or
                   x      |      y
                 _____

         b              c            a
```

4. *a.* She checked out a novel by Saul Bellow

b. She checked out a VW service manual

c. _____

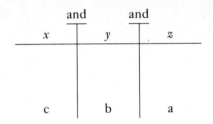

Introduction Exercise 1

In the list that follows you will find ten sets of assertions, each accompanied by a diagram showing the chunking of the relations. Using a separate sheet of paper, copy each diagram and code in the letters of the assertions. Then write the sentences of each set in logical order, including (where you feel they are needed) the signal words provided or other appropriate signal words. (For sets 6 through 10, you will have to supply your own signal words.)

Example:

a. Marge was frantic

b. The cat hadn't shown up for two days

c. Marge was worried

Here *b* is the cause and *a* and *c* the effect, so *b* is coded in the first blank. "Frantic" is an intensification of "worried," so *c* is coded in the second slot and *a* in the third:

a. Marge was frantic

b. The cat hadn't shown up for two days

c. Marge was worried

"The cat hadn't shown up for two days. Therefore, Marge was worried. In fact, Marge was frantic."

1. *a.* The dog had got out of the house
   b. Jerry left the screen door open
   c. The kitchen was full of flies

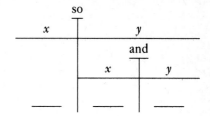

2. *a.* On the horizon were massive cumulus clouds
   b. The weatherman had promised clear weather
   c. On the horizon were thunderheads

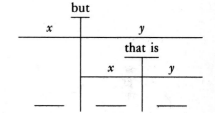

3. *a.* Western Samoa has two main islands
   b. One is Upolu
   c. One is Savaii

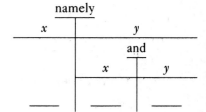

4. *a.* She bought some bait
   b. She bought some fishhooks
   c. She bought some nightcrawlers

5. *a.* I didn't study for the test
   b. I went out for a walk
   c. I didn't work on my term project

6. *a.* I didn't study for my test
   b. I feel guilty
   c. I didn't work on my term project

effect		cause
	coordinate	coordinate
___	___	___

7. *a.* His face appeared slowly over the back of the sofa
   b. It was a round white face
   c. It looked like a full moon rising

comparison		comparison
complex	component	
___	___	___

8. *a.* He straightened the living room
   b. He cleaned the kitchen
   c. He scrubbed the kitchen floor

coordinate		coordinate
includer	included	
___	___	___

9. *a.* We discreetly left them alone
   b. Jeff and Ann were having a fight
   c. Jeff and Ann seemed to be having a fight

cause		effect
assertion	regression	
___	___	___

10. *a.* She got up
    b. It was 7:30 A.M.
    c. She stoked the fire in the potbellied stove

time		assertion
	coordinate	coordinate
___	___	___

Introduction Exercise 2

In the following sets the diagram establishes how the assertions are related. But for each set one assertion is missing. On a separate sheet of paper write out the entire set, including your own *c* assertion for each set, according to the relations chunked in the diagram.

Example: *a.* We could have green beans
b. We could have broccoli
c. _____

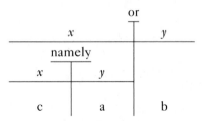

We see that the missing assertion is the includer for the coordinate assertions "we could have green beans or we could have broccoli." Here are some possible options for *c*:

"We had a choice between two green vegetables."
"We could choose between my two favorite vegetables."
"We were faced with the unpleasant choice."
"They offered us vegetables."

Suppose, though, that the same two assertions *a* and *b* were in this diagram:

We could have what we'd had yesterday.

Now the *c* assertion is the includer for *a* only. Here would be some options:

"We could have what we'd had yesterday."
"We could have the vegetable I could not stand."
"We could have my favorite vegetable."

Here, then, are some sets to work on.

1. *a.* We could have green
     beans
b. We could have broccoli
c. _____

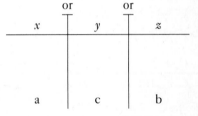

2. *a.* We could have green
   beans
   b. We could have broccoli
   c. _____

	or	
x		*y*

or		
x	*y*	

| a | b | c |

3. *a.* We could have green
   beans
   b. We could have broccoli
   c. _____

operation	stages	
	coordinate	coordinate

| a | b | c |

4. *a.* The bird alighted on the
   fence
   b. The bird tipped forward
   briefly
   c. _____

coordinate	coordinate	
	operation	stage

| c | a | b |

5. *a.* The bird alighted on the
   fence
   b. The bird tipped forward
   briefly
   c. _____

operation	stage	
	operation	phase

| a | b | c |

6. *a.* The bird alighted on the
   fence
   b. The bird tipped forward
   briefly
   c. _____

	or	
x		*y*
	comparison	comparison

| a | b | c |

7. *a.* The brakes screeched shrilly
   b. The car pulled to the curb
   c. _____

	coordinate		coordinate
operation	stage		
b	a		c

8. *a.* The brakes screeched shrilly
   b. The car pulled to the curb
   c. _____

operation		stages	
	coordinate	coordinate	
b	c		a

9. *a.* He bought a used car
   b. He brought a Ford
   c. _____

	namely			
x		y		
		namely		
		x	y	
a		b		c

10. *a.* The blades were dull
    b. We found two problems with the lawnmower
    c. _____

	namely			
x		y		
		and		
		x	y	
b		a		c

We have just looked at a few one- and two-level patterns for chunking the discourse relations we studied in Part I. And later we'll look at a few more. But we need to recognize a simple fact first: the number of possible chunking patterns—of even four or five levels—is almost unlimited. And, of course, the pattern for a piece of discourse only a few pages long may have over a hundred levels, and it may be different from any other pattern ever used. In short, even in a book much longer than this we could not expect to cover all possible patterns of chunking the discourse relations.

Still, there are some fairly basic patterns of discourse relations that characterize certain types of discourse. We need to look at two basic types of discourse, each of which has two basic subtypes. We need to see first that the types differ in their basic *purpose*: to *depict* or *explain*. We need to see second that certain discourse relations and patterns will be more useful for explaining, certain others for depicting.

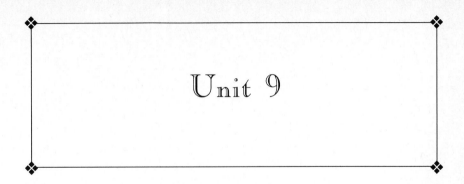

Unit 9

Purposes of Discourse

Most of the writing we do in college has one of two general purposes: to depict or to explain. **Depictive** writing is what might be called presentational, or sensory. Its purpose it to *depict* an object or an action, to make it come alive to our senses. With depictive writing we see, hear, taste, smell, and otherwise sense what is there or what is happening. **Explanatory** writing, on the other hand, is basically logical: its purpose is to *explain* concepts or beliefs. Of course, no sharp line absolutely separates depiction from explanation, but as you work through this section you'll get a feel for the difference between, say, *depicting what* is happening and *explaining why* something happened or should happen. They are different enough, and serve sufficiently different purposes, that it's worth our time to treat them separately.

Depictive writing is itself of two sorts: **Description** and **Narration**. When we depict a static object or scene, we are *describing*. We might describe a car sitting at a curb (its color, the condition of the paint, the crumpled left fender). Or we might describe a tree on a calm day, a photograph of a crowded beach in midsummer, or the contents of our refrigerator. When we depict a static object or scene (one that for the moment is not changing), we are writing description.

The relationships of most value to us are the whole/part, comparison/ comparison, and place/assertion relationships.

Narration, by contrast, involves our depicting an activity—an object or scene that is changing even as we depict it. We might narrate the action of a car pulling away from a curb (the squeal of the tires, the gravel kicking up and spraying a man crossing the street, the grinding sound as the driver shifts gears). Or we might narrate the action of a tree swaying in the wind, the activity of an actual beach scene on a midsummer afternoon, or the process of getting all the fixings for a submarine sandwich from the refrigerator. Narration uses operation/stage or phase, manner/assertion, comparison/comparison, and time/assertion to best advantage.

Depictive writing, then, is called *description* when it depicts a static scene, *narration* when it depicts an activity, that same scene changing in time and space.

Explanatory writing can also be divided into two types: **Exposition** and **Persuasion**. When we are concerned merely with explaining *what we know* about a subject, we are writing exposition. When we are concerned not merely with explaining what we know but also *how we feel* about a subject, we are writing persuasion. If your task is to explain what steps are followed when a doctor performs the procedure we call an abortion, explaining those steps would be expository. But if your purpose is to argue for or against legalized abortion, such an argument would be persuasive.

Thus, we have four sorts of writing: two depictive (description and narration) and two explanatory (exposition and persuasion). If you wanted to depict an empty baseball stadium on a warm summer evening, you would use your senses to create a *description* of what you see, smell, hear, and so on; if you wanted to depict the activity of a baseball game in the same stadium, you would use your senses to create a *narration* of the action; if you wanted to explain the rules of the game of baseball, your explanation would be simple *exposition*; if you wanted to argue, say, the superiority of the game of baseball over the game of football, you would be writing *persuasion*.

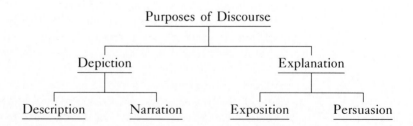

Of course, the four sorts of writing won't always be as pure and distinct as our classification might suggest. For one thing, narration almost always involves at least some static description, and description may well involve some action. (The static scene of the baseball stadium might include the activity of papers blowing across the empty infield; the narration of the baseball game might include a static picture of the ivy-covered right-field wall or the shadow of the grandstand across the third-base side of the diamond.) Even an expository account of the history of baseball might include the description of a famous baseball stadium (say, Yankee Stadium or Ebbetts Field) or the narration of a particularly exciting World Series game or the argument that certain rule changes have made the game less exciting. But as long as we recognize that the four sorts of writing—though not totally separate at all times—represent four largely separate *purposes*, our classification will be useful.

The following patterns (like the four sorts of writing they represent) are intended not to be entirely separate and rigid but merely to be useful, instructive. They are designed to help you write description, narration, exposition, and persuasion. But, again, when you use the pattern designed for, say, narration, recognize that (1) it is not the only pattern one might use to write narration and (2) features of that pattern may also work on occasion with other sorts of writing. As long as you look at these patterns as *possibilities*, not as restrictions or stipulations, they will have served their purpose.

Before we look at each mode of writing in turn, we need to consider the three sorts of awareness that govern the way we perceive (and therefore write about) the reality we live in. We'll call these three sorts of awareness *sensation*, *logic*, and *emotion*.

It's not always easy to separate these three sorts of awareness. In fact, much if not most of our writing is a subtle, shifting blend of the sensory, the logical, and the emotional. But to help us control these three sorts of awareness in our writing, it is useful to try to separate them.

To show how subtle the differences are that separate sensation from logic from emotion, let's take the single occasion of music playing on a radio. The sounds that you hear—the notes and voices that impinge on your consciousness—are sensation, *sensory* information. If you think to yourself, "That's guitar music, and it sounds like Parkening is playing a baroque piece," you've made some *logical* interpretations. And if, finally, you feel deeply moved by the music—sad, say, or inspired, or elated—you would be responding *emotionally*.

In a later exercise you will be asked to choose the most purely *sensory* term from among four terms. In order to do this, you have to see the predominantly *logical* and *emotional* qualities of the other terms.

As a preview of that exercise, classify the members of the following sets of terms as sensory, logical, and emotional.

1. *a.* a *majestic* tree   *b.* a *pine* tree   *c.* a *gnarled* tree
2. *a.* a *buzzing* sound   *b.* an *intermittent* sound   *c.* an *irritating* sound
3. *a.* *fear*   *b.* *a tightening in the stomach*   *c.* *a reaction*
4. *a.* The room was *upstairs.*   *b.* The room was *humid.*   *c.* The room was *pleasant.*
5. *a.* a *burning* feeling   *b.* a *different* feeling   *c.* an *angry* feeling

Depictive Writing

Description

How might we describe a tree? We might go from the whole (tree) to a part or parts (branch, trunk, leaves). We might go from the whole (tree) to a quality or qualities (bent, stunted, towering). Or we might go from an assertion (The tree was shaped flat against the wall) to a comparison (The shape was like a candelabrum).

These three ways of sharpening a static picture—looking at a part of the whole, looking at a quality of the whole, or making a comparison—work at more than one level. Just as we can focus on part of a tree (say, a branch), so we can focus on part of a branch (say, a twig) or parts of a twig (say, leaf buds) or on a quality or qualities of the leaf buds (shiny, bronze-colored leaf buds) or a comparison of those qualities (like shiny beetles lining each twig). In other words, these relations are reusable in any plan for describing a static scene or object.

It is important to remember that reusable patterns can work in either direction. The tree was our original whole. But can you think of a situation where the tree could be a part? If we coupled the assertion "There was a tree" with the assertion "It was an attractive building site," the tree would be a part, the building site the whole. And the building site might itself be a part of grandpa's farm. And the farm could be a part of the valley, and so on.

Exercise 9.1

The following are sets of descriptive sentences, each set accompanied by a pattern showing how the sentences might relate. Write out the sentences in the sequence suggested by each plan. Be prepared to discuss the effects of other patterns.

Example:

a. She was wearing white rubber boots
b. The raincoat was patterned with little green frogs
c. She was wearing a rainhat
d. She was wearing a raincoat
e. She was dressed for the rain

whole	parts		
			and
	x	y	z
		whole	part
e	a	d	b	c

"She was dressed for the rain. She was wearing white rubber boots. She was wearing a raincoat. The raincoat was patterned with little green frogs. And she was wearing a rainhat."

1. a. There was a hamburger
b. There was a cup of coleslaw
c. He stared indifferently at his lunch
d. There was a serving of French fries

whole	parts		
			and
	x	y	z

The next set builds on the previous one. Note what additions have been made. Be prepared to discuss other options for chunking these same assertions.

2. a. There was a hamburger
b. There was a cup of coleslaw
c. He stared indifferently at his lunch
d. There was a serving of French fries
e. The French fries were limp
f. The French fries were white

whole	parts		
			and
	x	y	z
		whole	qualities
			and
		x	y

*For simplification, certain combining has already been done. For example, here the qualities "white" and "rubber" have been added to "She was wearing boots."

Again, the next set builds on the previous one. Note the changes. Again, what other sequences might we use for these same assertions?

3. *a.* There was a hamburger
   b. There was a cup of coleslaw
   c. He stared indifferently at his lunch
   d. There was a serving of French fries
   e. The French fries were limp
   f. The French fries were white
   g. The cup was waxed paper
   h. The hamburger contained a piece of lettuce
   i. The hamburger contained a thin patty of meat
   j. The hamburger contained a slice of tomato

whole	parts						
	x		y		and z		
whole	quality	whole	qualities and		whole	parts and	
			x	y		x	y	z

Here is one final expansion of the previous set. After you have arranged all the assertions in the pattern suggested, ask yourself how that pattern might still be expanded. For example, where could the following assertion go? "There was a thin milkshake." What further expansions could you make from that assertion?

4. *a.* There was a hamburger
   b. There was a cup of coleslaw
   c. He stared indifferently at his lunch
   d. There was a serving of French fries
   e. The French fries were limp
   f. The French fries were white
   g. The cup was waxed paper
   h. The hamburger contained a piece of lettuce
   i. The hamburger contained a thin patty of meat
   j. The hamburger contained a slice of tomato
   k. The tomato slice was like Styrofoam
   l. The French fries were like partially cooked pasta
   m. The tomato slice was pithy
   n. The lettuce was wilted
   o. The tomato slice was pale pink

whole	parts					
			and			
	x		y		z	
whole	quality	whole	qualities	whole	parts	
			assertion	comparison	and	
			and		x	y	z
			x	y	whole	quality	whole	qualities
							and
							x	y
							assertion	comparison

5. *a.* There was a window
   b. The table had a bowl of fruit
   c. The chair had a cushioned seat
   d. The room was pleasant
   e. There was a table
   f. The window had bright pink curtains
   g. The chair had a straight back
   h. The table had a vase of daffodils
   i. There was a chair
   j. The chair had curved legs

whole	parts					
				and		
	x		y		z	
	whole	parts	whole	part	whole	parts
		and				and
		x	y	z			x	y

As an additional exercise, add sentences making *fruit* more specific. Add sentences naming two qualities of the daffodils.

Exercise 9.2

Depictive writing is *sensory*. It depicts what our senses—sight, hearing, touch, and so forth—tell us about the world outside our heads. Each of the following sentences has a blank, to be filled by *one* of the words or phrases in parentheses. Copy each sentence, filling the blank with your choice of word or phrase—the word or phrase that *focuses most sharply on sensation*. Then be prepared to discuss which sense (smell, balance, taste, etc.) the word reflects. Your teacher may also wish you to discuss in what ways the other words fail to focus on sensation or why one term focuses more specifically or sharply on sensation than another.

The kitten was _____.
(a) Manx   (b) a young male   (c) soft and warm   (d) affectionate

Note that *all* the words or phrases help describe the cat. And note that we might use our senses to determine that the cat was Manx (we might *see* his stubbed tail or his longer rear legs) or a young male or affectionate. But only "soft and warm" suggests the *immediate* sensation of touching our skin to his furry body.

June felt _____.
(a) angry   (b) out of place   (c) refreshed   (d) dizzy

Again, each word or phrase helps define how June felt, and "refreshed" *suggests* certain sensations (say, clean or cool after having been dirty or hot, or satisfied after having been hungry or thirsty), but only "dizzy" directly *names* an immediate, specific sensation (from the sense of balance).

1. Below the house was a _____ barn.
   (a) red   (b) recently painted   (c) cozy   (d) cow
2. He picked up _____ knife.
   (a) his brother's   (b) a shiny   (c) a hunting   (d) the steel
3. The party was _____.
   (a) nearly over   (b) highly successful   (c) crowded   (d) noisy
4. She handed me two yards of _____ cloth.
   (a) silky   (b) silk   (c) expensive   (d) patterned
5. Dave leaned back against the _____ bricks.
   (a) stacked   (b) adobe   (c) rough   (d) extra
6. We heard a _____ noise.
   (a) shrill   (b) irritating   (c) confusing   (d) constant
7. A(n) _____ odor greeted us.
   (a) pleasant   (b) familiar   (c) putrid   (d) aromatic
8. The _____ fish glinted in the bright sunlight.
   (a) hooked   (b) thrashing   (c) struggling   (d) frightened
9. _____ blew across the alley.
   (a) Some trash   (b) Something   (c) A candy wrapper   (d) A waxy brown paper

10. We could hear _____coming from the room.
    (a) noises   (b) whispering sounds   (c) hissing whispers   (d) ominous whispers
11. It tasted _____.
    (a) strange   (b) like clams   (c) delicious   (d) suspicious
12. A _____ jacket was hanging on the back of the chair.
    (a) crimson   (b) red   (c) brightly colored   (d) bright crimson

It's time for you to try on your own to bring together everything we've discussed about descriptive writing—how we sharpen a static picture by focusing our senses in turn on parts or qualities or resemblances (comparisons).

❖———————————————————————❖

Essay Assignment Two
Northbound (Gregory Strachov)

Option 1   On the cover of the text is a reproduction of an original watercolor by Gregory Strachov, entitled *Northbound*. Consider it a static scene, one you are to *depict (describe)* in words. Divide the scene into parts and subparts. Find *sensory* qualities to describe and comparisons to make. For example, you might describe the shape or color or texture (quality) of one of the stones (part) by saying what it resembles (comparison).

Option 2   The following listed sentences are intended merely to get you started on a description. Using whole/part, whole/quality, assertion/comparison, place/assertion* and coordinate/coordinate, create a detailed picture starting with one of the listed sentences.

For each picture you do, let the sentence you have been given represent only the *whole*. Use your senses to choose parts and parts of parts, to choose qualities, to choose comparisons. And make sure you are *actually using your senses* as you do this assignment. (It's important if the whole is, say, "I looked through the glass at the jewelry display" that you *actually look at a jewelry display* when you write your parts and qualities and comparisons. Don't *imagine* a scene; *observe* it.)

a. Suddenly I became aware of the sounds in the room.

* You may choose not to use full assertions to locate your other assertions in space. Simply be aware that a phrase such as "in the corner" or "above the pork roasts" is used to *locate* your assertion, to place it relative to the other wholes and parts.

b. I looked through the glass at the _____.
  (jewelry display, array of meats, florist's display, etc.)

c. They were the familiar odors of _____.
  (a hospital, a rest home, a pet store, a bar, a pizza parlor, etc.)

d. I lay _____. (in the hot sun, on the rumpled bed, in the sand, in the shallow water, etc.)

Narration

Narration is like description in that for both sorts of writing we use our *senses* to *depict*. With description we depict a static scene. With narration we depict an *activity*. With description we look from the static whole to the static parts. With narration we look from the whole activity to *subactivities—what the parts are doing*.

It is useful to recall our distinction between two sorts of "parts" of an activity. One sort we called "stages"; the other sort we called "phases." Stages are the sort of parts that follow one another in sequence. The movements of a symphony, the innings of a baseball game, the class hours in your college day are all stages. Phases are the sort of parts that go on at the same time. What the violins are doing and what the woodwinds are doing at the same moment would be phases of a symphony. The batter's activity, the pitcher's activity, and the first baseman's activity might be phases of the same play in the first inning of the baseball game. One stage must end before a coordinate stage begins, but phases are activities that can go on simultaneously.

Exercise 9.3

Examples of two paired relations—activity/stages and activity/phases—appear in the following list. Decide in each case whether the included elements are coordinate *stages* or coordinate *phases* of an activity (operation).

Examples: a. dinnertime / preparing the meal, eating the meal, cleaning up
  b. dinnertime / eating, conversing, listening to background music, sipping coffee

Note that example *a* is basically activity/stage. The meal is prepared in stage one, consumed in stage two, and cleaned up after in stage three. It's possible for there to be some overlap (Don may clear his plate—part of cleanup—before Sam has finished eating), but for the most part each stage ends before the next begins.

In example *b*, on the other hand, each little subactivity of the main activity "dinnertime" can overlap or interrupt another: one person can be doing two or three at once (even if it's considered questionable manners to converse with a bite of salad in your mouth). So the activity "dinnertime" in *b* has been divided into *phases*, subactivities that can go on at the same time.

Here are some to practice on.

    1. a. running a mile on a track / breathing deeply, pumping the arms, taking long strides . . .

       b. running a mile on a track / running lap one, running lap two, running lap three . . .

    2. a. doing the wash / gathering the dirty clothes, putting them in the tub, starting the cycle . . .

       b. doing the wash / the action of the agitator, the movement of the clothes in the water, the hum of the motor . . .

    3. a. Simon and Garfunkel, "The Concert in Central Park" / "Mrs. Robinson," "Homeward Bound," "America," "Me and Julio" . . .

       b. Simon and Garfunkel, "The Concert in Central Park" /Steve Gadd's drumming, Anthony Jackson's bass work, Paul Simon's guitar work, Art Garfunkel's singing . . .

    4. a. calling home / talking to Mom, doodling, lying on floor, tapping foot . . .

       b. calling home / dialing, listening to ring, saying "hello," asking Dad how Mom is . . .

    5. a. gardening / planting the beans, planting the corn, planting the radishes, planting the carrots . . .

       b. gardening / growth of the beans, growth of the corn, growth of the radishes, growth of the carrots . . .

Just as with description, narration offers three ways to sharpen our depiction of an activity: (1) we can focus on a detail—a stage or phase ("He ran, *his arms pumping furiously*"); (2) we can name a quality, or manner ("He ran *with jerky motions*" or "He ran *smoothly*"); or (3) we can make a comparison ("He ran with jerky motions, *like a badly lubed robot*"). And as place/assertion helps locate what we're depicting in a description (static), so time/assertion helps locate what we're depicting in a narration (active).

Exercise 9.4

Following are ten paired sets of sentences, the *a* set establishing a relationship for you to use to complete the *b* set. First, decide what relationship the second sentence of *a* bears to the first sentence (a stage or phase, a quality, a comparison). Then use the same relationship to create a sentence to fill the blank in *b*.

Example: *a.* She paced nervously. Her rubber soles squeaked with each step.

             b. He fidgeted at his desk. _____

First, what relationship does "Her rubber soles squeaked with each step" bear to "She paced nervously"? *Pacing* is the whole activity (or operation). The squeaking of her soles is part of that activity (either a phase or stage— we can't know which without adding a *coordinate* stage or phase). So to complete "He fidgeted at his desk," we would need to concentrate on a *stage* or *phase* of that fidgeting. We might fill the blank with something like this: "His fingers drummed rapidly on his English text"; or "He scuffed the floor with his left heel"; or "He shifted his weight from one hip to the other every few seconds."

1. *a.* She stared at Fred. It was an unblinking stare.
   b. He smiled. _____
2. *a.* She stared at Fred. Her stare was like that of a bird of prey.
   b. He smiled. _____
3. *a.* She stared at Fred. Her pupils shrank to tiny dots of black.
   b. He smiled. _____
4. *a.* He cleaned up the highchair tray. He brushed the crumbs with his hand.
   b. She revved the dirt bike. _____
5. *a.* Darla ran the water for the dishes. She squeezed a thin ribbon of soap under the running water.
   b. The cat curled up in the doorway. _____
6. *a.* The storm front approached. Wind soughed through the pine branches.
   b. Pedestrians surged into the crosswalk. _____
7. *a.* He tapped his forehead with his thumb. It was as if he were tipping an imaginary hat.
   b. Rex thumped his tail against the floor. _____
8. *a.* Laura strode into the meeting. She strode briskly.
   b. The van tipped as it rounded the curve. _____
9. *a.* He stroked his beard. The stroking was gentle.
   b. She shook her head. _____
10. *a.* The stroking was gentle. It was as if he were stroking a sleeping infant.
    b. The shake was almost imperceptible. _____

Sets 9 and 10 in the previous exercise suggest the structure of the next exercise. Note that 9a and 10a combine to form a sequence: "He stroked his beard. The stroking was gentle. It was as if he were stroking a sleeping infant." The chunking pattern would be:

activity	quality
comparison	comparison

The following exercise builds narrative sequences by combining these relations: activity/stage, activity/phase, activity/quality, or manner, comparison/comparison, and coordinate/coordinate.

Exercise 9.5

Three sets of sentences to combine into narratives are in the following list. A chunking plan accompanies each set. (Remember that the chunking plan given isn't necessarily the only way to combine the sentences in the set. It's just the way you're asked to do it.) On a separate sheet of paper, copy the chunking pattern, code in the sentences, and combine them according to the chunking pattern. Be prepared to discuss other options for chunking these same assertions.

    1. a. Ted vacuumed the carpets
       b. Carl washed the dishes
       c. They hurried to clean the apartment
       d. Andy cleaned the bathroom
       e. Carl took out the garbage

activity	phases		
		and	
x	y		z
	and		
	x	y	

    This set builds on the previous one. When you copy the chunking plan, notice what additions have been made. Take your time coding in the sentences in order to see how the previous plan has increased in complexity. Then combine the sentences according to the chunking pattern. Be prepared to discuss other options for chunking these same sentences (assertions).

    2. a. Ted vacuumed the carpets
       b. Carl washed the dishes
       c. They hurried to clean the apartment
       d. Andy cleaned the bathroom
       e. Carl took out the garbage
       f. The washing of the dishes was hasty
       g. Andy wiped up the tile floor
       h. The vacuum motor droned steadily through each room

activity	phases				
			and		
	x		y		z
		and			
activity	phase	x	y	activity	stage
		activity	quality		

Again this set builds on the previous one. Complete this set as you did the previous one, noting other chunking patterns you might use. In addition, see how you might add even more levels to the pattern (say, by adding an *x or y* within the second comparison chunk, stating another resemblance for the sound of the vacuum.

3. *a.* Ted vacuumed the carpets
   b. Carl washed the dishes
   c. They hurried to clean the apartment
   d. Andy cleaned the bathroom
   e. Carl took out the garbage
   f. The washing of the dishes was hasty
   g. Andy wiped up the tile floor
   h. The vacuum motor droned steadily through each room
   i. Andy scrubbed the toilet
   j. The vacuum sounded like an enormous bumblebee
   k. The washing of the dishes was careless
   l. Andy cleaned the tub

activity	phases						
				and			
	x		y		z		
			and				
activity	phase	x	y	activity	stages		
							and
	comparison	comparison		assertion	qualities		x	y	z
					and		
					x	y	

Exercise 9.6

The following are three chunking diagrams for a three-stage narrative *you* are to write. The initial sentence (the operation, or activity) will be provided. Add sentences of your own to fill out the diagram. Each diagram requires you to add to what you have already written.

Example: 1. *a.* Brenda prepared to study for her exam
     b. _____
     c. _____
     d. _____

activity	stages		
			and
	x	y	z
a	b	c	d

The first diagram tells us that "Brenda prepared to study for her exam" in three stages—*x*, *y*, and *z*. Let's fill those stages this way: *(b) First, she fixed herself a snack*; *(c) Then she put a Jean Redpath tape on the tapedeck*; *(d) Finally she opened her text.*

Keeping what we have already written, let's sharpen the narrative by adding other relations:

Example: 2. *a.* Brenda prepared to study for her exam
     b. She fixed herself a snack
     c. She put a Jean Redpath tape in the tapedeck
     d. She opened her text
     e. _____
     f. _____
     g. _____

activity	stages						
						and	
	x				y		z
					and		
	activity	stages		x	y		
		and					
		x	y				
a	b	e	f	c	g		d

The new diagram tells us that "She fixed herself a snack" is now an activity with two stages of its own—*e* and *f*. Let's have those stages be "She made a peanut-butter sandwich" and "She poured a glass of buttermilk." Likewise, *c* ("She put a Jean Redpath tape in the tapedeck") is now the first stage of a two-stage activity. So *g* will be a *coordinate* stage. Let's let *g* be "She turned the tape on low."

Our entire narrative so far reads:

"Brenda prepared to study for her exam. First she fixed herself a snack. She made a peanut-butter sandwich. And she poured a glass of buttermilk. Then she put a Jean Redpath tape in the tapedeck. And she turned the tape on low. Finally she opened her text."

One more installment in our example and it will be time for you to develop your own narrative.

Example: 3. *a.* Brenda prepared to study for her exam
   b. She fixed herself a snack
   c. She put a Jean Redpath tape in the tapedeck
   d. She opened her text
   e. She made a peanut-butter sandwich
   f. She poured a glass of buttermilk
   g. She turned the tape on low
   h. _____
   i. _____
   j. _____
   k. _____

activity	stages									
								and		
	x					y		z		
							and			
	activity	stages				x	y	activity	quality	
					and				comparison	comparison
		x			y					
		activity	stages							
				and						
			x	y						
a	b	e	h	i	f	c	g	d	j	k

Note what we are asked to add this time. The stage "She made herself a peanut-butter sandwich" is now an activity with two coordinate stages. Write two sentences that would be coordinate stages of making a peanut-butter sandwich. Also, "She opened her text" is now an activity that we must name a *quality* of. *How* (in what *manner*) did she open her text? Write a sentence that names a quality of her act of opening the text. Finally, make a *comparison* to sharpen that quality. If she opened her text "slowly," write a sentence that compares how slowly: "It was as if. . . ."

Now it's time for you to repeat this three-stage process using your own activity. The following list has several topics that could serve as the initial *activity* sentence for a brief narration. Choose one that names an activity you can actually observe and report on. (Remember that narration, like description, is depictive: you must use your *senses* to depict the activity in your narration.) Then write three narratives based on that activity, each narrative adding to the previous one. The first will follow chunking diagram 1, the second chunking diagram 2, the third chunking diagram 3. You may, of course, add narrative relations *beyond* those called for in each plan (for example, your activity may have four or five coordinate stages instead of only three), but be sure that your narrative has all the relations called for in each chunking diagram.

Incidentally, each activity sentence has "I" as the subject. If you wish to observe the activity as an outsider, make another person (a *he* or *she*) the subject.

"Activity" sentences for narratives:

a. I cleaned up the kitchen after dinner.
b. I donated a pint of blood.
c. I spent the rest of the hour playing [an electronic game].
d. I shaved.
e. I put on my makeup.
f. I mowed the lawn.
g. I got a fire started in the fireplace.
h. I brewed a cup of tea.
i. I fixed the flat tire.
j. I arranged the flowers.
k. I baited the hook.
l. I cut the pineapple.

❖———————————————————————————❖

Essay Assignment Three
Narrating from Personal Observation

Choose a place on campus (the bowling alley, dorm, commons, gymnasium, quad, ballfield, etc.) where you can record an activity. Using full sentences, record the activity, its stages, phases, substages, qualities. Use comparisons to sharpen the picture. Be sure you focus on sensory information (especially on what you can see and hear) rather than on your feelings or on background information.

Explanatory Writing

As we have just seen, the purpose of depictive writing is to depict an object (description) or an activity (narration)—to make that object or action come alive to the senses. The purposes of explanatory writing, by contrast, are to *inform* and to *persuade*. Writing whose chief purpose is to inform (explain, define) is called *expository*, or *exposition*. Writing whose purpose is not only to explain but to persuade (argue, convince) is called *persuasive*, or *persuasion*. We are now ready to examine some plans (chunking patterns) that characterize these two sorts of explanatory writing.

Exposition

If I depict a particular collie lying on a specific braided rug in front of a certain fireplace on a given winter's evening, I am writing description. But if I *define* the characteristics of collies in general, explaining the color subtypes and defining the differences between collies and other breeds of dog, I am writing exposition. If I depict an ebony-skinned eighteen-year-old girl in the act of styling her hair in front of the softly steamed bathroom mirror, I am writing narration. But if I explain in detail the steps and substeps one takes to create a corn-row hairstyle, I am writing exposition.

Obviously, it is not the subject matter that determines whether I'm writing depiction or exposition; it is my *handling* of that subject matter. Depiction is concerned with making an object or action come alive to the senses. Exposition is concerned with *defining* or *explaining* a thing or activity. And please keep in mind that one way of handling the subject matter is neither better nor worse than another way. Each way is legitimate. Each way reflects your *purpose* at that time.

We might contrast depiction and exposition this way:

Depiction	*Exposition*
1. Immediate, here-and-now detailing of a *particular* object or event.	1. Generalized explanation or definition of *typical* objects or events.
2. Concerned primarily with *sensory* information: touch, taste, hearing, sight, etc.	2. Concerned primarily with *logical* relationships: cause/effect, contrast/contrast, general/specific, etc.

An illustration should help. The following two passages deal with a human vertebra (one of the twenty-four movable bones in the spinal column). Read the two passages and determine which is *describing* (depiction) and which is *explaining* (exposition):

A. Each vertebra has a somewhat cylindrical bony portion (the body, or centrum), a number of spinous processes—usually three—and a bony arch, through which the spinal cord (the body's largest nerve trunk) passes from the brain stem (the medulla oblongata) to the lowest lumbar vertebra.

B. He picked up the vertebra, surprised at how light it felt, and turned it slowly. It was like a biscuit in color, heft, and size, and in shape too, except for three spurs of bone, thin, bladelike fingers splaying from the back, radiating from a dime-size hole. He held the bone close to his eye, sensing the faint odor of formaldehyde and decay, and could see—where the central bladelike finger was chipped—the fine latticework of the marrow inside, an amber geometry like honeycomb candy.

Let's assume that you (correctly) identified passage *A* as exposition and passage *B* as depiction. What evidence helped you make that choice? First, in *A* we are learning about vertebrae *in general*; in *B* we have a *particular* vertebra (one, as it happens, with a chip in that central "spinous process" that lets us look inside). Second, in *A* we do not feel, smell, or see a *real* vertebra; rather, we learn *general* defining characteristics about all vertebrae. In *B*, by contrast, we handle, smell, and look carefully at one specific vertebra: we notice its weight, shape, color (all "like a biscuit"), smell the formaldehyde and decay, look inside at the amber latticework of the bone marrow. Again, the point is this: the *subject* is not what distinguishes depiction from exposition; rather, it is one's *treatment* of the subject. Each treatment reflects a different *purpose*.

Exercise 9.7

Following are four chunking patterns and four paired sets of assertions, each paired set combined according to the same pattern. First, match each pair with the correct pattern. Then determine which set of the pair is depiction (narration or description) and which is exposition.

A.

whole	parts		
		and	
x	y		z

B.

general	specific		
		and	
x	y		z

C.

operation	stages or phases		
		and	
x	y		z

D.

whole	qualities		
		and	
x	y		z

Sets   *1. a.* The following procedure is recommended for washing white clothes. First, fill the tub with hot water. Second, add soap and bleach. Third, add the clothes.

   b. Denise prepared to barbecue. First she piled the charcoal briquets in a rough pyramid. Then she doused them liberally with starter fluid. Finally she touched a brightly flaring match to the lower tier of briquets.

2. a. The cages housed several birds. One small cage contained a pair of rice birds. A tall cage with a dead tree sheltered a sparrow hawk. Three bright-green parakeets preened in a glass-enclosed cage.

   b. One family of birds is known as raptors. Raptors include hawks. Raptors include owls. Raptors include eagles.

3. a. He leaned closer to the narcissus bloom. It was delicate. It was white. It was richly fragrant.

   b. One byproduct of the process is alcohol. Alcohol is colorless. Alcohol is volatile. Alcohol is toxic.

4. a. The eye is a three-layered structure. The outermost layer is the sclera. The middle layer is the choroid. The innermost layer is the retina.

   b. The squirrel draped limp in Blue's jaws. One leg hung by a thread of tendon. The eyes were glassy. Blood flecked the grey fur.

Exercise 9.8

We have just used four includer/included patterns to help distinguish depictive writing from expository writing. We are now going to use them in generating *exposition*.

For each chunking pattern, or plan, there will be three sets of assertions. The first set has all four assertions; you need only arrange them to fit the chunking pattern. The second set has one or more assertions missing; you are to supply the missing assertion(s). The third set you are to generate on your own, selecting a topic from those listed or choosing your own topic.

1A. 1. The grasshopper has a head
   2. The grasshopper is a typical insect
   3. The grasshopper has an abdomen
   4. The grasshopper has a thorax

whole	parts		
		and	
	x	y	z
___	___	___	___

  B. 1. The kettledrum is included in the percussion section of most symphony orchestras
   2. It has a hollow hemisphere of copper or brass
   3. _____
   4. It has a series of tuning pegs for stretching the top

whole	parts		
		and	
	x	y	z
1	2	3	4

  C. 1. _____
   2. _____
   3. _____
   4. _____

whole	parts		
		and	
	x	y	z
1	2	3	4

(Possible structures include a flower, the human heart, an automobile tire, a blouse, a notebook. You may add coordinate parts beyond three if you wish.)

2A. 1. The walnut is native to North America
   2. The pecan is native to North America
   3. Several deciduous nut-bearing trees are native to North America
   4. The shagbark hickory is native to North America

general	specific		
		and	
	x	y	z
___	___	___	___

B. 1. Fur-bearing mammals figured significantly in the opening of the American West

2. Fur-bearing mammals include the otter

3. _____

4. _____

general	specific		
		and	
	x	y	z
1	2	3	4

C. 1. _____

2. _____

3. _____

4. _____

general	specific		
		and	
	x	y	z
1	2	3	4

(Possible topics include communist governments, situation comedies, drugs, religions, videogames, tropical fish, rocks, stars, rock stars. You may add coordinate specifics beyond three if you wish.)

3A. 1. The adult butterfly emerges from the cocoon

2. The butterfly begins life as an egg

3. A cocoon housing the developing winged adult constitutes the pupal stage

4. The life cycle of the butterfly is complex

5. The caterpillar marks the stage of greatest growth

operation	stages			
			and	
	w	x	y	z
____				

B. 1. _____

2. The calf is firmly secured

3. The hot branding iron is pressed into the hide

4. A disinfectant/ointment is applied to the burn

operation	stages		
		and	
	x	y	z
1	2	3	4

C. 1. _____

2. _____

3. _____

4. _____

operation	stages or phases		
		and	
	x	y	z
1	2	3	4

(Possible topics include break dancing, fly tying, baking bread, studying for an exam, playing handball, trying a court case, throwing a frisbee, debating, swimming the butterfly, cleaning a birdcage. You may add coordinate stages or phases beyond three if you wish.)

4A. 1. Mozart's music is balanced
 2. Mozart's music is elegant
 3. Mozart's music is true classical music
 4. Mozart's music is regular

whole	qualities		
		and	
	x	y	z
___	___	___	___

B. 1. A Boy Scout is expected to be of good character
 2. A Boy Scout is expected to be loyal
 3. _____
 4. _____

whole	qualities		
		and	
	x	y	z
1	2	3	4

C. 1. _____
 2. _____
 3. _____
 4. _____

whole	qualities		
		and	
	x	y	z
1	2	3	4

(Possible first sentences would be "The Middle East situation remains tense"; "Summers in the Mojave desert are harsh"; "Leather is a common material for shoes"; "It is a highly nutritious soup"; "A good doctor has a certain personality." You may add coordinate components beyond three if you wish.)

We have just seen that four basic includer/included relations (general/specific, whole/parts, operation/stages or phases, and whole/qualities) can serve as patterns for expository writing. In fact, *all* the relations we learned about in Part I can serve in expository patterns. But rather than develop patterns using all combinations of the *x/y* relations (which would give us thousands of three-level patterns alone), we will focus on just a few more of the major expository patterns. The next set will be variations of cause/effect.

Cause/Effect 1

cause	effects		
		and	
	x	*y*	*z*

There are occasional times when we see a single cause as having more than one effect:

"The national debt is now at a record high. One result is that interest rates are rising. A second result is that American goods cost more abroad. A third result is that investors are becoming increasingly edgy."

(Note, incidentally, that matters might be a good deal more complicated than our simple chunking pattern suggests. For instance, in the example given above the investors might be getting edgy not only because the national debt is at an all-time high but additionally because the interest rates are rising and because of the fact that American goods cost more abroad. In other words, the pattern works even when it oversimplifies the facts.)

Cause/Effect 2

causes			effect
	and		
x	*y*	*z*	

Sometimes we attribute a single effect to more than one cause:

"The school lunch program has its largest budget ever. Social Security costs are at an all-time peak. And Medicare/Medicaid expenditures are greater than ever before. The result is that our national debt is now at a record high."

(Again, you might note some possible oversimplification here. For example, even if all the separate facts we have here are true, some might still be missing. Milk subsidies and tobacco price supports, for example, might figure in this record-high national debt. Loans to foreign countries or our own military spending might also. Try to list *all* of the causes you can for each effect.)

Cause/Effect 3

cause			effect

Sometimes a cause/effect relation becomes the cause for another effect, and that one for still another:

"The snowpack in the Rocky Mountains was at record levels that winter. The result was an extremely high spring runoff. This runoff left much low-lying agricultural land under a foot or more of water through most of May and June. As a consequence, 65 percent of the winter wheat crop was totally destroyed."

Cause/Effect 4

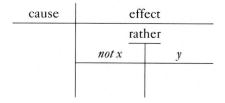

Sometimes the effect is not what one would expect. The expected effect is usually stated first, for contrast:

"Again the grid was electrically charged. But this time the rat did not try to avoid the shock. Instead, he simply stood there trembling."

Cause/Effect 5

Sometimes we examine evidence (effects of an unnamed cause) and conclude the probable cause (conclusion).

"The sleeping nests were still green and fresh. The broken ends of the bamboo shoots they had fed on were still oozing sap. The tracks in the mud had not been obliterated by the downpour two nights earlier. The gorillas had definitely stayed there last night."

Cause/Effect 6

possible cause(s)			known effect(s)
	and		
x	*y*	*z*	

Sometimes we guess the possible cause or causes of a known effect.

"Perhaps she felt her game slipping. Perhaps she wanted to quit a winner. Perhaps she just wanted to spend more time with her husband and children. Whatever the case, she retired that year from professional track."

Exercise 9.9

Following are the diagrams for the six cause/effect patterns we just looked at. For each you are given one or more assertions that fit the pattern. You are to create additional assertions to complete the pattern. Then choose your own subject and use the pattern again. Use a separate sheet of paper for your work.

Cause/Effect 1

1. *a.* A devastating tornado hit northern Ohio
   b. _____
   c. _____
   d. Power was knocked out for over half the state

cause	effects		
		and	
	x	*y*	*z*
a	b	c	d

First, fill in a *b* and a *c* assertion for the set above. Then write four more sentences using your own subject.

Cause/Effect 2

2. *a.* Tanya has a final tomorrow morning
   b. _____
   c. _____
   d. We've decided to reschedule tonight's meeting

causes			effect
	and		
x	*y*	*z*	
a	b	c	d

First, fill in a *b* and a *c* assertion for the set above. Then write four more sentences using your own subject.

Cause/Effect 3

3. a. _____
   b. Temperatures were in the mid-twenties overnight in many of the citrus-growing areas
   c. _____
   d. The price of Florida orange juice is expected to double within two months

		cause	effect
	cause	effect	
cause	effect		
a	b	c	d

First, fill in an *a* and a *c* assertion for the set above. Then, write four more sentences using your own subject.

Cause/Effect 4

4. a. The team ran back onto the field
   b. But _____
 * c. In fact _____
   d. Instead _____

*Notice that we've added a relation not in the original pattern, but one you should remember from Part I. Fill in *c* if you can. If you can't, go on to *d*.

cause	effect		
		rather	
	not x	y	
	indeed		
	x	y	
a	b	c	d

First, fill in a *b*, *c*, and *d* assertion for the set above. Then, write four more sentences using your own subject.

Cause/Effect 5

5. a. _____
   b. _____
   c. _____
   d. Ms. Reyes is an excellent teacher

evidence			conclusion
	and		
x	y	z	
a	b	c	d

First, fill in the *a*, *b*, and *c* assertions for the preceding set. Then, write four more sentences using your own subject.

Cause/Effect 6

6. a. Maybe the oven was too hot
   b. _____
   c. _____
   d. _____

possible causes			known effect
	and		
x	y	z	
a	b	c	d

First, fill in the *b*, *c*, and *d* assertions for the preceding set. Then, write four more sentences using your own subject.

A few more expository patterns and we'll be ready to move on to persuasion.

	problem	solution
contrast	contrast	

One of the most useful patterns in the type of exposition that we call "scientific" writing—expository writing concerned with problem solving—is represented by the pattern just shown. The overall chunking is problem/solution. The "problem" stage is created by a tension between two opposites, a contrast/contrast relation. The rest of the paper (usually the bulk of the paper) is devoted to resolving that problem. Following are some variations of this plan:

problem		solution
what we know	what we don't know	

Sometimes we know, say, *how* a certain phenomenon occurs or occurred (and we might spend a few paragraphs reviewing what we know). But we don't know *why*. After establishing that we don't know why it happens, we would attempt in the "solution" stage to tell why it happens.

problem		solution
data that make sense	data that don't make sense	

Sometimes we have evidence that supports a certain conclusion and evidence that doesn't support that conclusion. The conflict is resolved (solution) usually by reinterpreting the evidence or by coming to a different conclusion.

problem		solution
what some believe	what others believe	

Sometimes two different groups will look at the same set of facts and come to different conclusions. The solution comes in resolving the differences, normally by showing that one group has misinterpreted the facts.

Exercise 9.10

Read the first few paragraphs of several "scientific" articles (*Scientific American* would be a good magazine to try), and see if you can find the problem/solution pattern at work. See also if you can find variations in the "problem" stage that were not mentioned previously (for example, "what we expected to find" versus "what we found").

❖───❖

Essay Assignment Four
Introducing an Expository Essay

The following are the opening paragraphs to three different expository essays* (coded by letter and numbers for convenience). Each set of paragraphs is preceded by several questions, which you are to answer as you read. (Your teacher may ask you to write out the answers or simply to be prepared to discuss your answers in class.)

After you have read each set, let *one* serve as a model for you to use in developing your own opening paragraphs for an essay on a different subject. You need not follow the model slavishly; you need only be aware of the overall chunking pattern used by the model and in some way use that chunking plan yourself.

The main purposes of this exercise are two: first, obviously, to give you further practice in recognizing different chunking patterns for expository discourse and, second, to increase your sensitivity to what the audience, the reader, faces in trying to discover at the start what an essay is about.

*These essays appear in *NOVA: Adventures in Science*, produced by WGBH, Boston, and published by Addison-Wesley Publishing Company.

*Questions
to Essay A*

1. Read the following two paragraphs one sentence at a time, asking yourself at the end of each sentence: "What do I know so far about what subject the author intends to cover?" "How does this sentence relate to what went before?" "What relation might the next sentence have to what I've read so far?"
2. At what point do you feel that both the subject and the intended development of that subject have been summed up?
3. If the discussion part of the article these paragraphs introduce is divided into three coordinate segments, what is the purpose of each segment?
4. Which title would you find most appropriate for the article these paragraphs introduce: "Fires in Switzerland and America"; "Why America Burns"; "Big Fires"; "Greed and Fire Tragedy"?

*Introduction to
Essay A*

I.   Once or twice a year, a big fire makes the news. The MGM Grand Hotel's casino in Las Vegas goes up in flames, and eighty-four people die. Downtown Lynn, Massachusetts, burns, and an extensive urban renewal project is lost. These are the spectacular fires, the ones the newsmagazines and the networks cover. But the media and the rest of us tend to forget that during each hour that the MGM Grand or the city of Lynn burned, 300 other fires raged throughout America. Each of those hours of fire cost the country one life, three serious injuries, and $2 million—and each year there are 8,760 such fire-hours, resulting in 12,000 deaths, 24,000 tragic and disfiguring injuries, $20 billion dollars of damage, and unimaginable misery and pain. The young, the old, and the helpless are the most likely victims. Unfortunately, the problem seems to be getting worse.

II.   The United States has more than its share of fires. The fire death rate in Switzerland, with its dense concentration of ancient buildings, is one-tenth as high as America's, and the fire chief of Zurich cannot remember losing an entire residential structure. Why are we so fire-prone? The answer, it seems, lies in ignorance, carelessness, and greed.

*Questions
to Essay B*

1. Read the following three paragraphs one sentence at a time, asking yourself at the end of each sentence: "What do I know so far about what subject the author intends to cover?" "How does this sentence relate to what went before?" "What relation might the next sentence have to what I've read so far?"
2. At what point do you feel that both the subject and the intended development of that subject have been summed up?
3. What does paragraph 3 suggest about how the article will be developed?

*Introduction to
Essay B*

I.   When we look into the sky on a clear, moonless night, the stars appear as bright white specks against a vast black canvas. And if we look through powerful telescopes, the surrealistic spirals and gaseous clouds of distant galaxies leap into focus against a backdrop of black. This broad expanse, often stretching tens and hundreds of light years between two celestial bodies, looks to be the ultimate void, a desert of silence and darkness.

II. But if we could turn a knob and adjust our eyes to see far beyond the rainbow of colors in the visible part of the spectrum—the radiation we know as light—we would see that space is not a black void at all. It is aglow with radiation. This radiation is so pervasive and of such significance that its discovery was the most important event in the study of cosmology in the past fifty years. It has yielded crucial information to scientists who ponder the creation of our universe, providing able support for the theory that it all started about 20 billion years ago with a Big Bang.

III. Its discovery is also a fascinating scientific detective story, in which astronomers and physicists used space-age equipment and techniques available only in the past two decades or so to make their observations and the· ·pplied well-established principles of physics to interpret them. Like ma.. breakthroughs in science, this one happened through a combination of careful planning and sheer luck, and because investigators, after initial reluctance, followed the trail of evidence even though it shattered some cherished assumptions along the way.

Questions to Essay C

1. Read the following six paragraphs one sentence at a time, asking yourself at the end of each sentence: "What do I know so far about what subject the author intends to cover?" "How does this sentence relate to what went before?" "What relation might the next sentence have to what I've read so far?"
2. At what point do you feel that both the subject and the intended development of that subject have been summed up?
3. Direct quotations involve certain conventions. Can you find the conventions for (a) showing that something has been *left out* of the quoted material and (b) showing that something has been *added to* the quoted material? (Hint, the second paragraph uses both conventions.)
4. Where has narrative been incorporated into this exposition?
5. Of the three sets of explanatory paragraphs you will have read (*A, B,* and *C*), two would seem to lend themselves better than the third to a *persuasive* handling of the material. Which two sets suggest persuasion and why? Why does the other set not seem appropriate for a persuasive article?

Introduction to Essay C

I. Eve DeRock, a teacher who lives in the heart of Oregon's commercial forest region, remembers vividly the day in March 1977 when an International Paper Company helicopter flew overhead and sprayed a herbicide known as 2,4,5,T throughout the valley. The company wanted to kill grass and underbrush and clear the land for a planting of trees.

II. "The grass died on my part of the valley as well as International Paper's," she said. "A week later, my cows began to drop their babies; they aborted. The fish died in the creek, and we found quail hens dead on their clutches and grouse that died with their young. And our dogs began to bring in slicks [aborted fawns] from the woods. I felt that I was sick from summer flu. . . . I didn't have a whole lot of strength. It got worse, until long into fall. My body became sore, and the inside of my body was sore, and finally, I came down with chills, fever, and convulsions.

III. Shortly before dawn on March 17, 1978, the clatter of helicopters filled the sky over the fishing village of Portsall, on the northwestern tip of the Brittany coast in France. Curious townspeople who headed outside were greeted with a pungent stench that left them short of breath. By the time they got down to the harbor, a two- or three-minute walk for most of them, their eyes were watering, their faces stinging, their heads aching. The air was filled with the smell of oil.

IV. In the early morning light, fishermen could see their boats moored in the harbor, tossing about on waves of black muck. Turning seaward to see where it was coming from, they looked out on a peculiar sight: although it was the time of spring high tides, when incoming surf was especially heavy, and although winds were blowing at near-gale force, the fishermen could see no whitecaps. The sea was black, covered with a blanket of oil that was gushing from a stricken supertanker, the AMOCO CADIZ.

V. One spring morning, a New Hampshire fish and wildlife worker was stocking streams and ponds with trout from the state's fish hatcheries. At one small lake, he was startled when a batch of young trout he had just released turned desperately back toward shore. They squirmed and writhed and seemed to gasp for air. Within minutes, they were dead, the apparent victims of acid rain.

VI. This is testimony from the forefront of the environmental crisis. Each incident, by coincidence, occurred in a setting far away from most of us—a rural forest, a foreign coast, a mountain lake—but the problems each portends are really no farther than the air we breathe, the water we drink, the food we eat. These and similar incidents have varying causes and effects, but they all have one common denominator: the oil (and other fossil fuels) manufactured by natural Earth processes over millions of years and now, through the magic of technology and chemistry, recovered and altered to serve the needs and convenience of humans.

Persuasion

When you write, it is always important to consider your audience—the person or persons you are writing to. The issue of audience is especially important when it comes to persuasive writing, because persuading different audiences calls for using entirely different approaches.

Any writer has three potential audiences for his or her argument: those who already share the writer's point of view, those who haven't made up their minds, and those who are already opposed to the writer's point of view.

For some reason many writers address only the first audience—those who already share their point of view. They ridicule and criticize the opposition; they assert that anyone holding beliefs that oppose their own must be stupid or immoral or both. Then they assert the wisdom and rightness of their own position.

Readers who already feel the way the writer does might be tempted to sit there nodding in agreement. But such an argument can be little more than a pep talk. It won't do anything to convince, to persuade, those who are skeptical of or opposed to the position being proposed. So let's agree that truly persuasive writing is more than just a pep talk or a rallying cry; truly persuasive writing is writing that changes the minds of those who are skeptical (the audience who haven't made up their minds) and of those opposed to the position being advocated.

To persuade those who are skeptical of or opposed to your opinion, you must do at least these two things: (1) *support your opinion* with reasons (evidence, facts) and (2) show that you *understand and respect the opposing opinion.*

Supporting your opinion requires that you supply the reasons (causes) for your opinion (effect). Thus, Persuasion Pattern One:

Persuasion Pattern 1

opinion	support		
		and	
	x	*y*	*z*

Let's assume that the rules governing the dormitory you live in allow dorm officials routinely to enter the rooms unannounced in search of illegal substances (alcohol, marijuana, etc.), disallowed equipment (electric hot plates, high-performance stereos, etc.), and evidence of vandalism or damage. And let's assume further that you believe such searches are wrong and should be stopped. If you want your opinion to convince those who hold no opinion or who hold the opposite opinion, you need to give some *reasons* in support. It is not enough merely to say, "Dorm officials should no longer conduct routine, unannounced searches of the dorm rooms." You must tell *why* you hold that opinion, and the *reasons* you give must do the convincing.

So the first thing you might do is jot down assertions that support your opinion—reasons for your coming to that opinion in the first place. Here are some you might have thought of:

1. My dorm room is my temporary home, where I should expect to have privacy.
2. The Constitution forbids government agents from search and

seizure without a court order. The same constitutional principles should apply to dorm officials.

3. By treating the dorm residents as untrustworthy, dorm officials
   may actually *encourage* them to break dorm rules.

Let's put these three support statements with our original opinion
statement (notice the additional assertions and the signals used):

> Dorm officials should no longer conduct routine, unannounced
> searches of the dorm rooms. First, our dorm rooms are temporarily our
> homes, and for someone to enter our homes uninvited is rude behavior,
> an invasion of privacy. I would not come unannounced to a dorm official's
> home and invite myself in to look around; I expect the dorm officials
> to treat my privacy with equal respect. Second, our Constitution forbids
> law enforcement officers from entering a private home and seizing prop-
> erty without a search warrant issued by the courts. The same constitu-
> tional principles should restrain officials from search and seizure in the
> dorms. Finally, if it is the intent of the dorm officials to reduce the
> breaking of dorm rules, the present search-and-seizure policy may actu-
> ally be making matters *worse*. People tend to respond to trust by being
> more trustworthy. People tend to respond to distrust and suspicion by
> being less trustworthy. The distrust reflected by the present policy may
> actually encourage many students who would otherwise abide by the
> dorm policies to go against them.

If, to convince the dorm officials that their policy was wrong, all
we needed to do was state our opinion and our reasons, the job
would now be done. But certainly the dorm officials had their own
reasons—perhaps very good reasons—for establishing the policy in
the first place. And even those in our audience who are merely
skeptical (not hostile) want to hear the other side of the argument
before making up their minds. So it's not enough to offer an opinion
and three reasons (even very good reasons) for that opinion. We
must meet the second requirement. We must show that *we understand
and respect the opposing opinion.*

One way to truly understand and respect the opposing opinion is
to argue *for* that opinion, using the first persuasion pattern. Let's
for the moment forget that we've taken a position against unannounced searches of the dorm rooms and instead assert and support
the opinion that such searches are necessary.

What are three reasons we might give to support the opinion that
dorm officials actually need to search dorm rooms on occasion without
advanced notice? One reason might be that dorm policy forbids the
use of certain equipment—electric hot plates and high-performance
stereos, for example—in the dorm rooms. Unannounced searches

might uncover such equipment. Another reason might be that dorm residents often damage the fixtures and furnishings in their rooms. Students would be less able to cover up such damage if a search came unannounced. A third reason might be that residents often try to sneak alcohol and other drugs into their rooms. A fourth reason is that dorm residents may try to sneak members of the opposite sex into their rooms.

Let's put this together in a paragraph, just as though this were the position we were taking: (You'll notice that again we've made a few additions and deleted one reason in producing the paragraph. Try to see how these additions relate.)

> Routine unannounced searches of the dorm rooms are necessary. For one thing, many parents depend on dorm officials to assure that members of the opposite sex will not be allowed in their sons' or daughters' rooms. For another, dormitory rules forbid the use of hot plates (which increase the danger of fire) and of stereos (which could disturb other residents) in the dorm rooms. Finally, state laws forbid the use of alcohol by minors and of certain other drugs by anyone. Only through unannounced searches of the dorm rooms can the university officials be certain that the parents' expectations, the university rules, and the state laws are being observed by each dorm resident.

Now if our task were simply to support the right of university officials to search dorm rooms unannounced, we'd have, in the preceding paragraph, a good opening paragraph. But our argument is *against* such a policy, and we already have a good opening paragraph stating that position. The function of our second paragraph is to show that we understand and respect the opposing position, not to *take* that position ourselves. So we can't use *both* paragraphs as though each represents our point of view, or else we'll sound like a split personality arguing with himself. We need the second persuasion pattern.

Persuasion Pattern 2

assertion	reassertion
	concession	response

Pattern 2 begins with an assertion. The assertion in pattern 2 is actually the first paragraph we wrote for pattern 1. The rest of pattern 2 calls for a reassertion (a restatement of the original position), which comes about in two substages—a concession and a response.

All this may sound pretty complicated (especially when we use terms like "assertion," "concession," and "response"). But the plan is something you've used before; only the names are new. Here's a picture of what we're talking about.

assertion	reassertion	
	but	
	concession	response
It was an enjoyable vacation	I admit that it was a little hectic	it was lots of fun

Exercise 9.11

The following are three pieces of discourse governed by persuasion pattern 2. Read them carefully and decide at which point each divides between assertion and reassertion and then at which point the reassertion divides into concession and response.

1. I don't like green salads. I realize they're good for me, but I just don't like them.
2. Terry is a good friend. Granted, he can be exasperating at times. He's almost always late for appointments. In fact, he often forgets them altogether. And he almost never answers the letters I write him. Nonetheless, he's totally open, totally loyal, and always ready to lend a hand or a dollar.
3. The fifty-five-mile-per-hour speed limit ultimately benefits us all. First, gas mileage decreases as speeds increase, so we burn far more fuel at seventy than at fifty-five. The more fuel our nation uses, the more economically dependent we become on other nations. And the more fuel our nation uses, the more we deplete for future generations the finite supply of fossil fuels. Second, the lower speed limit has reduced dramatically the number of traffic accidents and highway fatalities. States where the fifty-five-mile-per-hour limit is strictly enforced report a decline in traffic deaths of as much as 20 percent from the days of sixty-five- or seventy-mile-per-hour limits.

Of course many people find the lower limit too restricting. They feel particularly frustrated on the open stretches of highway in less populated areas, in many of the western states, for example. Truckers, whose income often relates directly to how rapidly they deliver the goods, are especially likely to chafe under the fifty-five-mile-per-hour limit. They want to be able to open their rigs up when the road is empty and straight or when they have to build up momentum for a grade. Finally, many people argue that today's vehicles and highways are designed for faster speeds than the current limit.

Still, the benefits of the fifty-five-mile-per-hour limit far outweigh the disadvantages. Conserving fuel is crucial if we are to maintain a degree of independence from foreign suppliers in the short run and husband the limited world supply in the long run. And, again, there is no arguing with the correlation between highway speed and traffic fatalities. In figuring the truckers' profits, the cost of one human life is difficult to calculate. Finally, it's true that today's vehicles and highways are safer at high speeds than the vehicles and highways of forty years ago. But, more important, they are safer *today* at fifty five than at seventy.

It's time to return to our argument regarding routine searches of the dorm rooms. We've already stated and supported the argument *against* such searches, and we've stated it as our own position. But the larger pattern (persuasion pattern 2)

assertion	reassertion	
	concession	response

requires that we look at the opposing opinion (concession) before we restate our own position (response).

Remember, though, that we must express the opposing opinion not as our *own* but as our opponents' opinion. Note how we have incorporated the second paragraph, which follows, as a *concession* paragraph, by putting the argument in the mouths of our opponents (the major additions have been underlined).

> *Of course, university officials may feel that* routine unannounced searches of the dorm rooms are necessary. For one thing, many parents depend on those officials to make certain that members of the opposite sex will not be allowed in their sons' or daughters' rooms. For another, dormitory rules forbid the use of hot plates (which increase the danger of fire) and of stereos (which could disturb other residents) in the dorm rooms. Finally, state laws forbid the use of alcohol by minors and of certain other drugs by anyone. Only through unannounced searches of the rooms, *university officials argue,* can they be certain that the parents' expectations, the university rules, and the state laws are being honored by each dorm resident.

Note that with the italicized elements included the paragraph is now ready to be incorporated into our own argument. Other signals you might find useful in introducing a "concession" paragraph are "Granted," "One might argue that," "Some people feel that," or "I recognize that," though with this last signal what you recognize can't *contradict* your argument.

Let's incorporate both paragraphs and write a final "response" paragraph, a paragraph that answers the points raised in paragraph two and reasserts the position taken in paragraph one. Our three-paragraph essay might read like this:

Dorm officials should no longer conduct routine, unannounced searches of the dorm rooms. First, our dorm rooms are temporarily our homes, and for someone to enter our homes uninvited is rude behavior, an invasion of privacy. I would not come unannounced to a dorm official's home and invite myself in to look around; I expect the dorm officials to treat my privacy with equal respect. Second, our Constitution forbids law enforcement officers from entering a private home and seizing property without a search warrant issued by the courts. The same constitutional principles should restrain officials from search and seizure in the dorms. Finally, if it is the intent of the dorm officials to reduce the breaking of dorm rules, the present search-and-seizure policy may actually be making matters *worse*. People tend to respond to trust by being more trustworthy. People tend to respond to distrust and suspicion by being less trustworthy. The distrust reflected by the present policy may actually encourage many students to go against dorm policies who would otherwise abide by them.

Of course, university officials may feel that routine unannounced searches of the dorm rooms are necessary. For one thing, many parents depend on those officials to make certain that members of the opposite sex will not be allowed in their sons' or daughters' rooms. For another, dormitory rules forbid the use of hot plates (which increase the danger of fire) and of stereos (which could disturb other residents) in the dorm rooms. Finally, state laws forbid the use of alcohol by minors and of certain other drugs by anyone. Only through unannounced searches of the rooms, university officials argue, can they be certain that the parents' expectations, the university rules, and the state laws are being honored by each dorm resident.

But one can sympathize with the university officials for the problems they face without necessarily endorsing their method of solving those problems. Granted that many parents expect university officials to keep their children separated from members of the opposite sex, at least in their dorm rooms. But shouldn't questions of "moral behavior" really be up to the students themselves at this point? Is it the function of the university officials—or the parents for that matter—to police the activities of eighteen-year-olds, who are legally young adults? Granted also that the university officials have an obligation to establish policies that will protect the safety and the comfort of the residents. But are unannounced dorm searches necessarily the best way to catch those who are risking fire with hot plates or who are disturbing their neighbors with stereos turned too loud? Certainly, if a few students break the rule forbidding cooking in the rooms, the cooking odors will give them away. And if a student can sneak a stereo into his room and keep it so quiet that no one hears it, he has obviously met the spirit of the rule against stereos, which is to keep from disturbing others. Granted, finally, the university officials should be constantly alert to evidence of the abuse of alcohol or other drugs among the residents. And certainly residents suspected of substance abuse should be counselled, and those obviously guilty of continued substance abuse should be put on probation or expelled. But wouldn't university officials accomplish *more* by a program aimed at educating young adults about the risks of substance abuse than they would by bursting unannounced into the dorm rooms in hopes of catching someone with a beer or a joint? In all, it seems to me that a policy built on sound educational principles and on trust will accomplish more than a policy based on suspicion and surprise tactics. Some residents will still betray that trust, but they are likely to feel the disapproval of their peers as much as that of the university officials.

That final paragraph is a long one, I recognize, but the plan is still fairly simple. The opening sentence serves as the opinion to be supported. The concession/response plan is then used in each of the coordinate "support" chunks (*granted x but y*). And the final two sentences serve as a generalization based on all three specific examples. The pattern used in the final paragraph looks like this (note the similarities and differences between this and the other two persuasion patterns):

Persuasion Pattern 3

opinion	support				
				in all	
	specific				general
		and			
	x	y	z		
	yet	yet	yet		
	true x	y	true x	y	true x	y

Before you write your own persuasive essay, let's review the chunking patterns once again. Pattern 2 gives the chunking for an entire three-paragraph essay (or four-paragraph, or seven-, or ten-): an assertion (stating and supporting your opinion), a concession (stating as sympathetically as possible the opposing point of view and even granting the merits of that point of view) and a response (restating your original position and responding to issues raised in the concession section). The other two patterns suggest a structure for the individual paragraphs (or chunks; the essay can be shorter or longer than three paragraphs): pattern 1 for the assertion and the concession chunks, pattern 3 for the reassertion chunk.

❖——————————————————————————❖

Essay Assignment Five
Persuasion:
Making Your Argument

Using the argument on unannounced dorm inspections as a model (though you needn't follow it slavishly), write a three-paragraph (or longer) argument on one of the following topics:

1. Young couples considering marriage living together first
2. Keeping "hopelessly ill" individuals on life-support systems
3. Whether grade-school students who fail to master the subject should be advanced if they're trying their hardest
4. State-run lotteries
5. [Your own choice of topic]

Introduction

In Part I we studied the *relations* that any two assertions might make with one another: *x including y*, *x so y*, *true x yet y*, and so forth. In Part II we looked at the sorts of chunking *patterns* these relations form when we put assertions together to make discourse.

Perhaps you'll remember an artifical restriction we put on our discourse in Part II: for the most part it was made up of full assertions, units capable of being punctuated as separate sentences. Now it's time to lift that restriction. We're ready now to see what choices are available when we put the patterned relations of Parts I and II into *structures*: parts of sentences, full sentences, and paragraphs. Let's begin with a rather long paragraph—a long paragraph made up of fairly short sentences. The paragraph is not as its author originally wrote it, but it contains, as well as I can execute, the original words, relations, and chunking patterns:

> (1) A domestic reporter graduates from general reporting. (2) Then the domestic reporter hops up the ladder to success toward a single specialty. (3) That specialty may be sports. (4) Or that specialty may be organized labor. (5) Or that specialty may be the stock exchange. (6) Or that specialty may be the State Department. (7) This is true of the domestic reporter even at his best. (8) A foreign correspondent, by contrast, is required to act on an assumption that is preposterous but exhilarating. (9) The assumption is that he takes all knowledge for his province. (10) And thus, the assumption is that he is at home in a textile mill. (11) The assumption is that he is equally at home in a political convention. (12) The assumption is that he is equally at home in a showing of abstract art. (13) The assumption is that he is equally at home in a proxy fight. (14) The assumption is that he is equally at home in a launch pad at Cape Canaveral.

Our paragraph has fourteen sentences (numbered for our convenience) and 161 words. The overall chunking pattern is contrast/contrast (*x by contrast y*). Read quickly through the paragraph again and see where it is you learn that the behavior of a domestic reporter is being *contrasted* to another sort of behavior.

You found in rereading the paragraph that you learned first about the contrast/contrast structure when you got to sentence 8, where you have the signal "by contrast," which clearly signals a contrast/contrast relation. (Had the signal been, say, "likewise," the relation announced would have been comparison/comparison and the remaining sentences would all have stressed the similarity between the domestic reporter and the foreign correspondent.)

Now let's see how the "paragraph" actually was structured by its author, Alistair Cooke, in his book *Alistair Cooke's America*:

> Whereas a domestic reporter, even at his best, graduates from general reporting and hops up the ladder to success toward a single specialty

(sports, organized labor, the stock exchange, or the State Department), a foreign correspondent is required to act on the preposterous but exhilarating assumption that he takes all knowledge for his province and is equally at home in a textile mill, a political convention, a showing of abstract art, a proxy fight, or a launch pad at Cape Canaveral. (p. 12)

The first thing you might notice is that the fourteen-sentence paragraph is this time *a single sentence.* You'll notice also that Alistair Cooke's version is shorter by half—81 words as opposed to 161. You'll notice also that his version has almost no needless repetition, which the paragraph certainly has. But for our purpose in Part III perhaps the most significant change has to do with where it is you discover that the overall relation is contrast/contrast. In the fourteen-sentence paragraph you discovered that fact in sentence 8 (sixty-four words into the text), when you read the phrase "by contrast." In Alistair Cooke's version, though, careful, well-trained readers discover that the overall relation is contrast/contrast *when they read the very first word*: "whereas."

Another way of saying this is that the relations and the chunking patterns of the two passages are essentially the same but the *structures* are different. The first passage uses fourteen sentences; the second uses one. The first passage uses seven sentences in the first chunk of the contrast/contrast relation; the second uses a structure we'll be calling a *subordinate clause*—not an independent sentence at all. The purpose of Part III is to give you some practice in recognizing and using the *structures* available to us when we chunk our assertions as discourse.

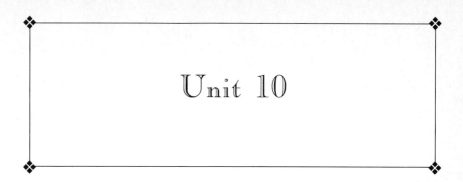

Unit 10

Structures of Coordination

The last of the relations we looked at in Part I was the relation we called coordinate/coordinate. The first structures we'll look at in Part III are called *structures of coordination*. Let's make clear at the start, though, that coordinate *structures* and the coordinate/coordinate *relation* are not the same.

For one thing, not all coordinate structures will be expressing the coordinate/coordinate relation. The *a*, *b*, and *c* structures that follow are called coordinate structures, but only one presents a coordinate/coordinate relation. Which is it?

    a. He shouted at the baby, and she started to cry.
    b. He fed the baby and started a wash.
    c. He fed the baby but forgot to change her.

Again, all three are coordinate *structures*, but only one is the coordinate/coordinate relation. The relation implied in *a* is cause/effect; we must assume that the baby started to cry *because* he shouted at her. The relation in *c* is contrast/contrast. Only in *b* is the coordinate structure expressing a coordinate/coordinate relation.

Not only will coordinate structures not always express the coordinate/coordinate relation, there are even times when a coordinate/ coordinate relation will be expressed in noncoordinate structures. In *d* and *e* below, the *relation* is coordinate/coordinate each time (*x and y*), but only sentence *e* expresses a *structure* of coordination.

> *d.* Angela appeared in court, along with her lawyer.
> *e.* Angela and her lawyer appeared in court.

Now that we've established what structures of coordination are not (that is, they're not *identical with* the coordinate/coordinate relations), let's see what structures of coordination are.

First, even in light of the caution just given, we can say that structures of coordination are in fact the structures that the coordinate/coordinate relations are *almost always* expressed in. Second, they are *grammatical* structures. So we're going to talk grammar for a moment.

The simplest sort of coordination occurs when we join what we've been calling "full assertions." The grammatical term for what we've called full assertions is *independent clause*, or *base clause*. We coordinate full base clauses in either of two ways: with a comma or with a semicolon. In edited writing the comma almost always has a coordinating conjunction following; the semicolon can be followed by a coordinating conjunction or a movable signal or by nothing besides the second (or subsequent) full base clause.

Since there are only seven coordinating conjunctions and since they ultimately account for most of our structures of coordination, let's memorize them. For ease of memorization, they have been classified as follows:

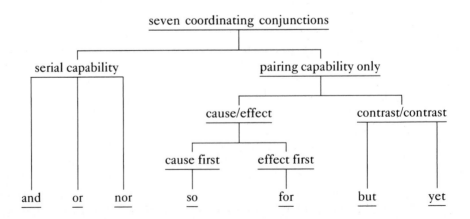

Exercise 10.1

On a separate piece of paper, copy the preceding classification diagram (it represents a logical chunking of the seven coordinating conjunctions). Then, to make sure that the classification diagram is meaningful to you, answer the following questions.

1. The seven coordinating conjunctions have been divided into two main chunks, on the basis of their ability to coordinate three or more items. Those that can coordinate three or more items are said to have "serial capability" (they can coordinate a *series*). Which coordinating conjunctions have serial capability? What, then, is meant by "pairing capability only"? Which coordinating conjunctions have pairing capability only?
2. Which two coordinating conjunctions are typically used to express the cause/effect relation?
3. Which two coordinating conjunctions are typically used to express the contrast/contrast relation?
4. Copy the following two sentences, filling in the blank with the logical coordinating conjunction. If the cause is stated before and the effect after, the conjunction will be *so*. If the effect is stated before and the cause after, the conjunction will be *for*.
   a. We rushed outside, _____ we could hear someone screaming.
   b. We could hear someone screaming, _____ we rushed outside.

The seven coordinating conjunctions can be used to join separate sentences (or paragraphs, or chunks of *any* size). But we're interested here in what happens when they join clauses *within the same sentence*. That is, how do we punctuate two coordinate clauses in the same sentence?

Coordination Rule 1

When we join two base clauses into a single sentence with a coordinating conjunction, we normally use a comma (,) or a semicolon (;) *before* the conjunction:

We couldn't get the car started, so we walked.

or

We couldn't get the car started; so we walked.

Exercise 10.2

In the list that follows you will find seven pairs of base clauses (independent clauses), each pair to be joined by one of the seven coordinating conjunctions. Join the pairs with the specified conjunction twice, using both punctuation options with each pair.

Example:

She couldn't leave the dog by himself } nor
She couldn't take him with her

She couldn't leave the dog by himself, nor could she take him with her.
She couldn't leave the dog by himself; nor could she take him with her.

1. *a.* Ms. Caldwell drives a Toyota } and
   b. Mr. Franklin drives a Dodge

2. *a.* You can buy a ticket at the university ticket office } or
   b. You can buy a ticket at the door

3. *a.* He couldn't make it to the stairway } nor
   b. He couldn't get back into his room

4. *a.* She yelled something } but
   b. I didn't hear what it was

5. *a.* Oil companies produce diesel fuel
      more cheaply than gasoline } yet
   b. They charge more for diesel fuel at the pump

6. *a.* She had developed fibrous tumors of the breast
   b. Her doctor recommended that she omit } so
      caffeine from her diet

7. *a.* He skipped breakfast } for
   b. He was late for work

Exercise 10.3

In the following list you will find seven base clauses and coordinating conjunctions. On a separate sheet of paper write out each base clause and coordinating conjunction. Then complete the logical relationships by writing your own *full* base clauses. When you join the pairs of clauses as a single sentence, use either a comma or a semicolon.

1. *a.* She bought a blouse for her mother } and
   b. _____

2. *a.* You may type your term papers } or
   b. _____

3. *a.* We didn't agree with what the speaker was saying } nor
   b. _____

4. *a.* Many indicators suggest that the economy is strong } but
   b. _____

5. *a.* They rehearsed the scene several times ⎱ yet
   b. _____ ⎰

6. *a.* Some of the children had forgotten their jackets ⎱ so
   b. _____ ⎰

7. *a.* I made a dental appointment this morning ⎱ for
   b. _____ ⎰

Besides using a coordinating conjunction to join two base clauses as a single sentence, we can join them in two other ways.

Coordination Rule 2

When we join two base clauses as a single sentence *without* using a coordinating conjunction, a semicolon will separate the base clauses. In such cases we sometimes join two independent clauses without any signal at all:

Marsha dropped all her classes; her sister continued at the university.

At other times we join two independent clauses with a *movable signal*. Note the punctuation.

Marsha dropped all her classes; *however*, her sister continued at the university.
Marsha dropped all her classes; her sister, *however*, continued at the university.
Marsha dropped all her classes; her sister continued at the university, *however*.

Exercise 10.4

In this exercise are seven sets of base clauses (independent clauses), to be joined as single sentences three times, in three separate ways: once with a coordinating conjunction, once with a movable signal, and once with no signal at all. Be prepared to discuss the different effects of these ways of joining the clauses. Choose your punctuation according to the rules already discussed, making certain that you use a comma *only if a coordinating conjunction follows*. Vary the position of the movable signal. For each of the last three sets you will have to choose an appropriate coordinating conjunction and movable signal.

1. *a.* The winters here are extremely harsh ⎱ and, moreover, [nothing]
   b. They last nearly six months ⎰

2. *a.* We could do the job ourselves
   b. We could hire it done
   } or, alternatively, [nothing]

3. *a.* I really love Mexican food
   b. It tends to give me gas
   } but, however, [nothing]

4. *a.* For three weeks there had been no rain
   b. They prepared to irrigate the corn
   } so, therefore, [nothing]

5. *a.* The total amount of energy in
      the universe remains constant
   b. The forms this energy takes can change
   } [you specify]

6. *a.* Arson investigators found physical evidence
      that the fire had been set intentionally
   b. They learned that two fire-insurance policies
      on the building had been purchased only
      weeks before
   } [you specify]

7. *a.* The blood pressure medication had
      unhealthy side effects
   b. She decided to control her blood pressure
      through diet and exercise
   } [you specify]

Practice with Deletion

So far in treating structures of coordination we have coordinated pairs of base clauses only—joining these pairs either with a coordinating conjunction (*and, but, or,* etc.) or a movable signal (*moreover, however, alternatively,* etc.) or nothing. But we won't always be coordinating full base clauses; sometimes we will join only part of one clause to another. And we won't always limit our coordinations to pairs of units; sometimes we will join three, four, or more units in a single series. Let's practice each in turn.

Even when we start with two base clauses, it's possible to combine them so that we end up with less. We do this by *deleting redundant information*—by removing needlessly repeated words. Let's see what options are available when we combine the following two assertions:

a. Controlling fire gave Neanderthals a source of heat
b. Controlling fire gave Neanderthals a source of light
} and

We can, of course, join these two clauses as we have others, using a punctuation mark and a coordinator—

Controlling fire gave Neanderthals a source of heat, and controlling fire gave Neanderthals a source of light.

But when we join them in this fashion, we see a great deal of redundancy—repetition.

We could also join them as base clauses with the punctuation and coordinator and yet still avoid some of the redundancy by substituting pronouns for some of the nouns or noun phrases:

> Controlling fire gave Neanderthals a source of heat, and *it* also gave *them* a source of light.

(The pronoun substitutes have been italicized. Determine what they replace.)

Even with these substitutes, though, we're still repeating a great deal of information. And we're still combining two full base clauses. Let's try combining these assertions so that we delete (leave out) the needlessly redundant information:

> Controlling fire gave Neanderthals a source of heat and light.

Notice that this option says just as much as the other two options, in fewer words. And notice that this result *requires no comma before the coordinator*.

Coordination Rule 3

When a coordinating conjunction joins two units that are less than full base clauses, we normally use *no* mark of punctuation before the conjunction: for example, "Controlling fire gave Neanderthals a source of heat *and* light."

Exercise 10.5

In the following list are five pairs of base clauses. Combine each pair three times, first as full clauses (use either punctuation mark before the coordinator), second as full clauses but with pronouns substituted for the repeated nouns or noun phrases, and third with only the new information coordinated (in other words, with all the needlessly repeated information taken out of the second assertion). You will need *no* punctuation before the coordinator with the third option.

Example:　　*a.* Johanna and I listed our complaints
　　　　　　　　b. Johanna and I presented our complaints to Professor Grimm $\Big\}$ and

　　　　　　　1. Johanna and I listed our complaints; and Johanna and I presented our complaints to Professor Grimm.
　　　　　　　2. Johanna and I listed our complaints, and we presented them to Professor Grimm.

3. Johanna and I listed our complaints and presented them to Professor Grimm.

1. a. My aunt seemed angry
   b. My aunt seemed in control } yet

2. a. The Amish counsel living a simple life
   b. The Amish disapprove of marrying outside the faith } and

3. a. Ramon removed the sheets from all the beds
   b. Ramon took the sheets from all the beds to the laundromat } and

4. a. Terrell will mail the report to Mrs. Pedroncelli
   b. Terrell will give the report to Mrs. Pedroncelli in person } or

5. a. My roommates won't be able to finish the chapter tonight
   b. My roommates won't be able to report on the chapter tomorrow } nor

There is one major exception to the rule we just looked at, an exception we noted in Part I. Sometimes less-than-full assertions joined by *or* need a comma. They do when the *or* signals the relation assertion/reassertion, or *x that is to say y*:

The aurora borealis, or northern lights, can't be seen at this latitude.

But notice that in this case we have a *pair* of commas setting off the entire reassertion at each end, not just separating coordinate assertions. And later we'll note that other pairs of marks besides commas can also be used.

Let's practice this exception to our coordination rule by combining two different relations: *x that is to say y* and *either x or y*. Only the *x that is to say y* relation will need punctuation. Sometimes it will require a pair of commas, sometimes only one. See if you can determine a rule.

Exercise 10.6

In the following list you will find six pairs of assertions relating either as *either x or y* or as *x that is to say y*. Combine each pair as a single sentence, deleting redundant information. In both cases the two assertions will be coordinated with *or*, but only the *x that is to say y* relation will require punctuation.

1. a. You'll need a coat
   b. You'll need a sweater } or

2. *a.* In every communication there will be some meaningless material ⎱ or
   b. In every communication there will be some "noise" ⎰

3. *a.* In every communication there will be meaningless material accompanying the message ⎱ or
   b. In every communication there will be "noise" accompanying the message ⎰

4. *a.* The majority of the voters are Republicans ⎱ or
   b. The majority of the voters are Democrats ⎰

5. *a.* She's a member of the Grand Old Party ⎱ or
   b. She's a Republican ⎰

6. *a.* These two-legged primate ancestors roamed the vast savannas of prehistoric Africa ⎱ or
   b. These hominids roamed the vast savannas of prehistoric Africa ⎰

In the preceding exercise the assertions relating *x* *that is to say y* can be handled in other ways than the one we have just practiced. For one thing, the *or* signal word can usually be removed (though it needn't be) without causing confusion. For another, two other pairs of marks can be used instead of the paired commas: a pair of parentheses, ( ), or a pair of dashes, —— —. As with the pair of commas, the second dash can be omitted if the element set off is the last in the sentence. The parentheses *always* work in pairs, even at the end of a sentence.

Exercise 10.7

In the list that follows you will find the four paired *x* *that is to say y* assertions from the previous exercise. Combine each set twice: once with the dashes (or a dash) setting off the *y* element, once with a pair of parentheses setting off the *y* element. Try leaving out the *or* at times. Note that if the parenthetic element closes the sentence, the period comes *after* the closing parenthesis.

Examples: *a.* The aurora borealis can't be seen at this latitude ⎱ or
   b. The northern lights can't be seen at this latitude ⎰

The aurora borealis—northern lights—can't be seen at this latitude.
The aurora borealis (or northern lights) can't be seen at this latitude.

1. *a.* In every communication there will be some meaningless material ⎱ or
   b. In every communication there will be some "noise" ⎰

2. *a.* In every communication there will be some meaningless material accompanying the message
 b. In every communication there will be some "noise" accompanying the message } or

3. *a.* She's a member of the Grand Old Party
 b. She's a Republican } or

4. *a.* These two-legged primate ancestors roamed the vast savannas of prehistoric Africa
 b. These hominids roamed the vast savannas of prehistoric Africa } or

Dual Modifiers

When two modifiers come before a noun, many writers have doubts about whether and how those modifers should be punctuated. In Essay Assignment Six we will look at at least four different types of dual modification and at the punctuation conventions signalling them.

Essay Assignment Six
Using Dual Modifiers

This is an exercise in punctuation conventions—punctuation *rules* as they're often called. The term *rules* is unfortunate, for at least two reasons. First, it suggests laws imposed on language from the outside (imposed, most innocent citizens suspect, by English teachers). Second, it suggests a certain inflexibility, as though for any language situation there is only one right way to do things.

The purpose of this exercise is threefold: (1) to show you that the rules (or conventions) are something we discover, something growing out of the efforts of speakers and writers to make their meanings clear, and not something imposed from the outside at all—not by English teachers or anyone else; (2) to provide you with data so that you can find out some of those rules for yourself—a process of scientific discovery; and (3) to give you the opportunity to communicate to others what you've learned, this through an expository essay, or report. All this is a tall order. And for that reason, this is a long exercise, the longest in the text. But for many students, this will be the most rewarding exercise, too.

Step 1   We'll start this exercise with four sentences, representing four different conventions of punctuation based on four different chunking relationships. These sentences are basic *data* to use in trying to determine the conventions. One word of caution before we start: these sentences are punctuated correctly (that is, according to established conventions), but *this is not the only way of punctuating any of these sentences.*

1. A short, rotund man strode into the room.
2. Most psychologists argue the existence of a short-term memory.
3. He held a short iron rod.
4. The word *catamaran* has three short (unstressed) syllables.

Let's look at each sentence in turn, noting its meaning and its underlying chunking pattern.

1. A short, rotund man strode into the room.

When we break the meaning of sentence 1 into its component assertions, we see these three:

A man strode into the room. The man was short. And the man was rotund.

What we notice is that the last two assertions are coordinate. In fact, they could be reversed, even in the original sentence (note that the punctuation remains the same):

A rotund, short man strode into the room.

Let's represent the chunking pattern of these coordinate (reversible) modifiers this way:

	x		*and*		*y*	
modifier	unit modified			modifier	unit modified
short	man			rotund	man

2. Most psychologists argue the existence of a short-term memory.

The underlying meaning of sentence 2 seems to derive from these two sentences:

Most psychologists argue the existence of a certain memory. That memory is short term.

What we see here is that *short* doesn't modify *memory*. Rather, it modifies *term*. And *short-term* as a unit modifies *memory*. The chunking pattern looks like this:

modifier		unit modified
modifier	unit modified	
short	term	memory

The use of the hyphen enables us to make a single modifier of *short* and *term*: short-term memory.

    3. He held a short iron rod.

Here the underlying meaning is best expressed by these two sentences:

    He held an iron rod. The iron rod was short.

In certain ways sentence 3 looks like sentence 1. In sentence 1, *short* and *rotund* both name qualities of the man. And in sentence 3, *short* and *iron* both name qualities of the rod. But here's a difference: *short* and *rotund* both modify *man* directly. They are coordinate and therefore reversible ("a short, rotund man"; "a rotund, short man"). But the modifiers *short* and *iron* are not coordinate. We can't comfortably speak of "an iron short rod." In the chunking pattern for sentence 3 *iron* modifies *rod*, and *short* modifies the two-word unit *iron rod*.

modifier	unit modified	
	modifier	unit modified
short	iron	rod

Note that when two modifiers assume this pattern, no punctuation is needed.

    4. The word *catamaran* has three short (unstressed) syllables.

The underlying meaning of this sentence is expressed by these two sentences:

    The word *catamaran* has three short syllables. That is to say, the word *catamaran* has three unstressed syllables.

The chunking pattern is this:

that is to say			
x		y	
modifier	unit modified	modifier	unit modified
short	syllables	unstressed	syllables

Note the punctuation we may use when the coordinate modifiers relate not as *x and y* but as *x that is to say y*: short (unstressed) syllables.

Here, then, are the four patterns and punctuation conventions you will write about. Read through them again if you have trouble remembering them. If not, move right on to step 2.

Step 2   Step 1 provided us examples of four basic sorts of dual-modifier relationships. In step 2 we will look at other examples of these same four relationships. Some of them use precisely the same punctuation conventions as the four examples we just looked at. Others use different punctuation, even though the relationships are the same.

Read the examples that follow, categorizing each according to the four punctuation patterns we just looked at. Notice especially those that use a different punctuation pattern. See if you can explain the alternative punctuation pattern in terms of what you have just learned. Notice also that 7 sentences (8 and 10 through 15) each represent more than one pattern.

1. She fixed him with a cold, baleful stare.
2. He was wearing an expensive leather jacket.
3. Jerry ordered the tuna-salad sandwich.
4. Don served the hot bread with sweet (unsalted) butter.
5. The rough-hewn log was maneuvered into place.
6. The President has several difficult and crucial decisions to make.
7. A cooling, gentle breeze came up late that afternoon.
8. Several carcinogenic, or cancer-causing, agents are present in cigarette smoke.
9. The shirt had large coffee stains.
10. She sat at an antique roll-top desk.
11. The school's success story is a child-designed, child-constructed play area.
12. He bought a dual-control king-size electric blanket.
13. An oval—egg-shaped—paperweight was in the box.
14. Several half-starved draft (work) animals drooped nearby.
15. They ordered the largest (eighteen-inch) and most expensive* ($13.95) pizza.

*You might notice that *most expensive* is a two-word modifier similar to that in the sentence-2 model, yet there is no hyphen. The convention is *not* to hyphenate

Technically, you now have the raw materials for your expository (explanatory) paper on dual modifiers. You have the four sentences representing four different sorts of dual modification. You also have chunking patterns illustrating each sort. You also have additional sentences representing the same and *alternative* ways of punctuating two sorts of dual modifiers. And the last six of those additional sentences (10 through 15) involve at least two sorts of dual modification each, so that you can talk about units within units (chunking). If you choose, you may skip the next section and go straight to Prewriting Essay Six. But if you'd like (or if your teacher would like for you to have) an additional challenge and an additional insight into how punctuation rules come about, then continue reading this section.

Within the last few years a new punctuation pattern for one sort of dual modifier has gained a foothold. It's so new that this may be its first mention in any textbook. So here's your chance to be a scientist of language —to look at the meaning and discover the chunking pattern of a fifth sort of dual modifier—a developing convention—and to incorporate that information into your paper. We'll take as a representative of this pattern sentence 5:

5. The USC/UCLA rivalry goes back years.

Here are five more examples to experiment with in discovering the chunking pattern. (Note that whereas *x and y* relates USC/UCLA, *x or y* relates one or more of these additional sentences. They've been numbered to extend our original list of fifteen sentences.)

16. The on/off switch is located on the back.
17. They used a mud/straw mixture for the bricks.
18. Such a threat normally triggers a flight/fight response.
19. He sometimes exhibits a Dr. Jekyll/Mr. Hyde personality.
20. She always takes an easy-come/easy-go attitude.

In defining this new dual-modifier relationship, you need to see in what ways it is similar to and different from the relationships we've already looked at. In some ways it resembles both relationships 1 (coordinate modifiers) and 2 (where the two modifiers are joined by a hyphen). In fact, each of the sentences above might appear with *both* hyphens *and* a coordinating conjunction:

They used a mud-and-straw mixture for the bricks.
Such a threat normally triggers a flight-or-fight response.

In what way or ways does this fifth pattern resemble relation number 1? (For example, try reversing the dual modifiers in number 5.) In what way

---

adverbials to the adjectivals they *clearly* modify: "fully equipped kitchen," "very tired child," and so on. But "fast-moving train" is an option. Can you see why? *Fast* could potentially modify *moving train*.

or ways does it differ from relation number 1? (Look for a difference in the chunking pattern. Can a mud/straw mixture be said to be either a mixture of mud or a mixture of straw separately in the same way that a short, rotund man can be said to be either a short man or a rotund man?) Likewise, in what way or ways does this fifth pattern resemble relation number 2? And in what way or ways do they differ?

Prewriting
Essay Six

All the exploration of dual modifiers done so far is part of the prewriting of Essay Six. But there is more you might do to explore the topic before actually writing the essay.

First you need to make as clear as possible to yourself (so that you can make clear to your reader) the *purpose* or *purposes* this essay is to serve. Spend a moment jotting down your purpose or purposes. (The purpose of fulfilling an English assignment for a grade can be assumed and doesn't count here.) If you have more than one purpose for this essay, then try to rank those purposes—primary, secondary, and so on. Having clearly in mind your goal (purpose) enables you to set subgoals and sub-subgoals more easily. (You might look at the second paragraph under Essay Assignment Six to see how I defined the purposes of the exercise.)

Second, define for yourself the sort of *audience* you're writing for. When I framed this long exercise, I was writing for a person who knew such matters as chunking and discourse relationships but was unsure when and how to punctuate dual modifiers. That's probably the best audience for you. Don't assume that you're writing for your teacher, who already knows what you're trying to say and who therefore might be counted on to interpret generously a few vague hints. You have to make this clear to someone who doesn't already know what you're trying to say.

Third, don't be too quick to follow the approach I used. I talked about five dual-modifier conventions, separating them into a set of four and a set of one. After all, my purpose was to create a choice of data for you to draw conclusions from, not to reach these conclusions for you. Your purposes might better be achieved by dividing these relations into, say, the set of coordinate relations and the set of noncoordinate relations. So experiment with different classifications of your five (or four) relationships.

Finally, don't be afraid to play with clusters or chains of relations, in the fashion of that early prewriting exercise you did with *Northbound*. And try freewriting the subject, letting the ideas flow in whatever direction just to get started. Good results can come from such apparently aimless exploration. In short, don't feel that before putting pen to paper you must see the essay whole. The first draft (and sometimes the second and even the third) *should* be in large part the act of discovering what it is you wish to say.

Exercise 10.8

In the previous exercise we found one sort of dual modifier using a hyphen:

Most psychologists argue the existence of a short-term memory.

Having seen hyphenated modifiers at work, we're ready to look at a special convention concerned with deleting redundant information. When two sentences are combined using hyphenated modifiers *containing the same word*, we can delete the repeated word, but it helps our reader if we don't delete the hyphen.

Example: Most psychologists argue the existence of a short-term memory $\Big\}$ and
Most psychologists argue the existence of a long-term memory

Most psychologists argue the existence of both a short- and a long-term memory.

Sometimes the extra hyphen can be deleted without causing too much confusion (as it might be in the preceding example). But sometimes, especially in a series of modifiers (the subject of our next section), the confusion that results from omitting the hyphen is very real. Notice what the following sentence seems at first glance to tell you:

The furniture has a chip, stain, and rust-resistant finish.

On first reading we perceive furniture with a chip and with a stain, until the third item requires us to go back and correct ourselves. Note how this version encourages us to hold the modifiers open till the end:

The furniture has a chip-, stain-, and rust-resistant finish.

Sometimes the repeated element comes before, not after, the hyphen. Let's see how that is handled:

It was a student-designed greenhouse $\Big\}$ and
It was a student-constructed greenhouse

It was a student-designed and -constructed greenhouse.

On a separate sheet of paper combine the following pairs of sentences, deleting the repeated word in the two-part modifier but using the hyphen to prevent misreading.

1. a. He is a city-born man $\Big\}$ and
   b. He is a city-bred man

2. a. The worker-owned business was a success $\Big\}$ and
   b. The worker-run business was a success

3. a. We chose the weather-proof siding $\Big\}$ and
   b. We chose the termite-proof siding

4. a. The three-year-old children were moved inside $\Big\}$ and
   b. The four-year-old children were moved inside

Series Coordination

All the structures of coordination (and the two noncoordinate modifying structures) we have looked at so far involved joining *pairs* of units, two chunks at a time. But the same principles can be applied, with certain adjustments, to the joining of three or more coordinate structures in a series (and to the noncoordinate modifiers as well). We'll look at some extensions of the principles developed so far.

First, of course, three or more full base clauses can be joined as a series in a sentence:

Megan played the violin; Salvador played the flute; and Willis played the oboe.

Usually we use semicolons for this purpose, though commas are also used, especially if the clauses are short. But it is important that the same mark be used throughout; *don't* start a series with one mark and switch to another:

* Megan played the violin; Salvador played the flute, and Willis played the oboe.

Second, we have the same option in combining three or more assertions that we have in combining two—the option of deleting redundant information. When we join two less-than-full assertions, we normally use no punctuation.

Mark is taking Math 100
Mark is taking History 105 } and

Mark is taking Math 100 and History 105.

But when we join three or more coordinate units in a series, we separate them with commas, normally using a coordinating conjunction to announce the last unit in the series.

Mark is taking Math 100
Mark is taking History 105 } and
Mark is taking English 101

Mark is taking Math 100, History 105, and English 101.

* The asterisk is sometimes used, as it is here, to signal a nonstandard construction.

Some writers omit the comma before the conjunction:

Mark is taking Math 100, History 105 and English 101.

Coordination Rule 4

When joining three or more chunks in a coordinate series, separate each chunk from the next with a comma or a semicolon. Use the same mark of punctuation throughout any given series.

Exercise 10.9

Combine the following six sets of assertions into coordinate series, deleting the redundant information. Be sure to separate each two units with a comma.

Example:

  a. Sharon can't attend the preliminary meeting
  b. Sharon can't attend the main session   } nor
  c. Sharon can't attend the special workshops

- Sharon can attend neither the preliminary meeting, the main session, nor the special workshops.

or

- Sharon can't attend the preliminary meeting, the main session, or the special workshops.

1. a. It was a cold morning
  b. It was a grey morning   } and
  c. It was a dreary morning

2. a. We could see two does
  b. We could see a buck   } and
  c. We could see three fawns

3. a. They could hold the meeting in the Presbyterian church
  b. They could hold the meeting in the high school gym   } or
  c. They could hold the meeting in the public library

4. a. You may have pie for dessert
  b. You may have cake for dessert
  c. You may have pudding for dessert   } and/or
  d. You may have fresh fruit for dessert

5. a. He didn't clean his room
  b. He didn't do the dishes
  c. He didn't mow the lawn   } or
  d. He didn't feed the dog

*6. a. The emu is a flightless bird
   b. The rhea is a flightless bird
   c. The ostrich is a flightless bird
   d. The penguin is a flightless bird   } and

The coordination we have been doing so far might be called one-level coordination. When we join two coordinate units, they are automatically on the same level:

We ate pizza and drank buttermilk
or
We drank buttermilk and ate pizza

And three or more units joined *in a series* are also on the same level:

My ears, feet, and hands felt chilled
My feet, ears, and hands felt chilled

But it is also possible for us to coordinate units at more than one level at a time.

The moa is an extinct flightless bird
The dodo is an extinct flightless bird   } and
The apteryx is an extinct flightless bird
The ostrich is an extant flightless bird   } [nothing]
The penguin is an extant flightless bird } and
The kiwi is an extant flightless bird

The moa, dodo, and apteryx are extinct flightless birds; the ostrich, penguin, and kiwi are extant flightless birds.

When we open up the possibility of pairs or series of units at various levels, we suggest possibilities of wondrous complexity. But the rules we have just rehearsed apply no matter how complex our structure becomes: when we join two units, we usually use only a comma *or* a conjunction, unless those units are full base clauses:

The bird fluttered and screeched
The bird fluttered, screeched
The bird fluttered, and it screeched

And when we join three or more units in a series, we separate them

* Note that changes beyond deletion must be made here—changes from singular to plural.

with semicolons or commas and the logical coordinating conjunction: "It is an expensive, dangerous, and rarely attempted process."

These rules apply no matter how many levels we're chunking:

> They were physically exhausted
> They were spiritually elated
> They were spiritually enthusiastic } and } but
> They were spiritually eager

They were physically exhausted but spiritually elated, enthusiastic, and eager.

Note that there need be no comma before *but*; the reason is that *but* joins only two chunks here and they are not both base clauses. What word would have to be repeated for *but* to be joining two base clauses?

Exercise 10.10

In this exercise you will find seven sets of units coordinating on two or more levels. Apply the rules of punctuation to join the bases at various levels of coordination into a single sentence. Feel free to substitute movable signals for the conjunctions. Feel free to experiment with pronouns. Be prepared to discuss different chunking sequences the sets might have.

Example:
   a. We are offering more attractive doors
   b. We are offering more attractive windows } and
   c. We are offering tighter-fitting doors
   d. We are offering tighter-fitting windows } and } and
   e. We are offering less expensive doors
   f. We are offering less expensive windows } and

We are offering more attractive, tighter-fitting, and less expensive doors and windows.

1. *a.* The wind howled
   b. The wind moaned } and } and
   c. The rain pelted down

2. *a.* Laura fed the dog
   b. Laura fed the cat } and
   c. Laura bathed the baby } and } and
   d. Michael fixed dinner

3. *a.* They cleared the fields
   b. They planted their crops } and
   c. They tended their crops } and
   d. They harvested their crops

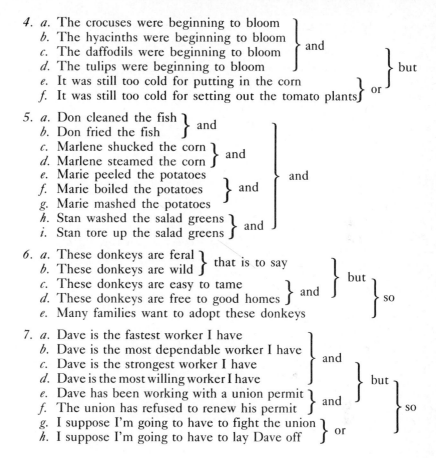

4. a. The crocuses were beginning to bloom
   b. The hyacinths were beginning to bloom
   c. The daffodils were beginning to bloom
   d. The tulips were beginning to bloom
   } and
   e. It was still too cold for putting in the corn
   f. It was still too cold for setting out the tomato plants
   } or
   } but

5. a. Don cleaned the fish
   b. Don fried the fish
   } and
   c. Marlene shucked the corn
   d. Marlene steamed the corn
   } and
   e. Marie peeled the potatoes
   f. Marie boiled the potatoes
   g. Marie mashed the potatoes
   } and
   h. Stan washed the salad greens
   i. Stan tore up the salad greens
   } and
   and

6. a. These donkeys are feral
   b. These donkeys are wild
   } that is to say
   c. These donkeys are easy to tame
   d. These donkeys are free to good homes
   } and
   e. Many families want to adopt these donkeys
   } but
   } so

7. a. Dave is the fastest worker I have
   b. Dave is the most dependable worker I have
   c. Dave is the strongest worker I have
   d. Dave is the most willing worker I have
   } and
   e. Dave has been working with a union permit
   f. The union has refused to renew his permit
   } and
   g. I suppose I'm going to have to fight the union
   h. I suppose I'm going to have to lay Dave off
   } or
   } but
   } so

Exercise 10.11

You will find in the following list three sets of base clauses, reflecting various punctuation options we considered in "Structures of Coordination." Combine each set as a single sentence, punctuating it according to those options. The base clauses may not be in the right sequence, so move them where you feel they belong when you combine them. Relations haven't been marked for you this time; you'll have to decide which signal words to use.

Example:

a. He was wearing a leather jacket
b. He was wearing a cowboy hat
c. The cowboy hat was ten gallon
d. The leather jacket was dark brown
e. The leather jacket was expensive
f. He was wearing cowboy boots

    g. The boots were alligator
    h. The boots were dyed blue

Possible combination:

He was wearing blue-dyed alligator cowboy boots, an expensive dark-brown leather jacket, and a ten-gallon cowboy hat.

1. *a.* He worked the dough with his fingers
    b. The dough was soft
    c. The dough was bread dough
    d. The dough was pliable
    e. The dough was slightly sticky
2. *a.* Sandra leaned against the wall
    b. Monica pulled the baby from the pool
    c. Sandra sobbed
    d. Sandra closed her eyes
    e. Monica placed the baby on her back
    f. Monica began gently puffing air into the baby's lungs
    g. Monica put her mouth over the baby's mouth and nose
3. *a.* Ishi used the blade to skin the buck
    b. The blade was long
    c. Ishi used the blade to slit the buck's throat
    d. The blade was obsidian
    e. The blade was volcanic glass
    f. The blade was razor sharp
    g. The blade was thin
    h. Ishi slung the buck from a branch
    i. The branch was low hanging
    j. The branch was thick

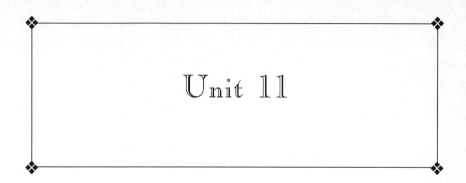

Structures of Subordination

The first structures we looked at—structures of coordination—are all by definition *grammatically equal to* any structure they directly relate to. Subordinate structures, again by definition, are *unequal to—grammatically dependent on*—the structures they directly relate to. This will make more sense as we look at examples.

The Subordinate Clause

In some ways subordinate clauses look very much like base clauses, especially a base clause joined to another by a coordinating conjunction:

a. They put away the tools, *for* it was nearly 5:00 P.M.
b. They put away the tools, *because* it was nearly 5:00 P.M.

You'll remember *for* as a coordinating conjunction (one, incidentally, that is fairly rare in modern discourse, its function having largely been taken over by *because*). What is the difference between the coordinator *for* and the subordinator (or subordinate conjunction) *because*? The difference is this: a subordinator *bonds with its clause*; a coordinator doesn't.

Bonds with its clause sounds a bit technical, but the meaning is simple. The simple translation is that we can say,

Because it was nearly 5:00 P.M., they put away the tools,

but we can't say,

* For it was nearly 5:00 P.M., they put away the tools.

Coordinating conjunctions always come *between* the base clauses (or any units) they coordinate:

They put away the tools, *for* it was nearly 5:00 P.M.
It was nearly 5:00 P.M., *so* they put away the tools.

Movable signals always come *between* the clauses they coordinate or somewhere *within* the second clause.

It was nearly 5:00 P.M.; *therefore*, they put away the tools.
It was nearly 5:00 P.M.; they put away the tools, *therefore*.

But subordinating conjunctions (subordinators) *bond* with their clause, taking it with them wherever they go.

They put away their tools, *because it was nearly 5:00 P.M.*
Because it was nearly 5:00 P.M., they put away their tools.

Because a subordinator bonds with its clause, it can move the clause around with respect to the base clause it relates to. The subordinate clause can come before the base clause:

Although we had arrived unannounced, Maria made us feel welcome.

Or it can come after the base clause:

Maria made us feel welcome, *although we had arrived unannounced*.

Or it can even interrupt the base clause:

Maria, *although we had arrived unannounced*, made us feel welcome.

Exercise 11.1

Eight pairs of base clauses are presented in the following list. They are to be joined by making one of the clauses a subordinate clause (by adding a subordinator) and joining it to the other. The subordinate clause may be placed *before* the base clause (in which case the subordinate clause will be followed by a comma). Or it may be placed *within* the base clause (in which case it will be set off by a pair of commas, parentheses, or dashes, one at each end). Or it may be placed *after* the base clause (in which case it will be separated from the base clause by a comma or by *no* mark of punctuation, whichever sounds better to you. Usually it will sound better without a comma). Remember that the subordinate and base clauses are *unequal, so you will not separate them with a semicolon or a period.* The subordinator is given for each pair of assertions, but you must decide which assertion it belongs with. In some cases it may go with either assertion. When it does, be prepared to discuss differences in meaning.

Example: The first week of January was extremely cold ⎫ because
             Natural-gas consumption increased sharply ⎭

Because the first week of January was extremely cold, natural-gas consumption increased sharply.

or

Natural-gas consumption increased sharply because the first week of January was extremely cold.

or

Natural-gas consumption (because the first week of January was extremely cold) increased sharply.

or

Natural-gas consumption increased sharply, because the first week of January was extremely cold.

1. *a.* Terry borrows my car
   b. He returns my car with the gas tank full ⎭ whenever

2. *a.* We tried for an hour to reach them by phone ⎫ although
   b. No one ever answered ⎭

3. *a.* I thought the plan was unfair ⎫ because
   b. I wrote a letter to the editor ⎭

4. *a.* He finishes by 6:30 P.M.
   b. It will be too late to pick up the flowers ⎭ even if

5. *a.* The sun was shining brightly
   b. They rolled out of their sleeping bags ⎭ when

6. *a.* The philodendron will die ⎫ unless
   b. He waters it soon ⎭

7. *a.* All parties involved will profit
   b. Tensions are eased in the Middle East ⎭ if

8. *a.* She worked hard all her life
   b. She managed to earn very little money ⎭ even though

We now have joined assertions using coordinators, movable signals, and subordinators. The following two exercises are intended as a review, to allow you to experiment and further familiarize yourself with these three sorts of signal words we have looked at so far.

Exercise 11.2

The following are four pairs of assertions relating as cause/effect. You are to join each pair at least six times, experimenting with coordinators (*for*, *so*), movable signals (*thus*, *therefore*, *consequently*, etc.), and subordinators (*because*, *when*, *since*, *in that*, etc.). See what happens when you change the order of the assertions. Mark with an asterisk (*) combinations that sound wrong or illogical.

Example: The cougar is an endangered animal   } cause/effect
It is illegal to hunt cougars in our state

- *a.* Because the cougar is an endangered animal, it is illegal to hunt them in our state.
- *b.* The cougar is an endangered animal, so it is illegal to hunt them in our state.
- *c.* It is illegal to hunt cougars in our state inasmuch as it is an endangered animal.
- **a.* It is illegal to hunt cougars in our state; consequently, it is an endangered animal.
- *e.* It is illegal to hunt cougars in our state, for it is an endangered animal.
- *f.* It is illegal, because the cougar is an endangered animal, to hunt cougars in our state.
- *g.* The cougar is an endangered animal; hence, it is illegal to hunt cougars in our state.

- *1. a.* He tore a hole in his rubber boot
  - *b.* His foot got soaked
- *2. a.* Tickets were $25.00 apiece
  - *b.* They decided to watch the game on television
- *3. a.* Her report was well received by the company president
  - *b.* She was offered a promotion
- *4. a.* Danny started to cry
  - *b.* His mother turned off the TV

We have just looked at three ways of signalling the cause/effect relation: using coordinators (*for*, *so*), movable signals (*therefore*, etc.), and subordinators (*because*, etc.). These same three types of signal work also for concession/response (though of course different signal words will be needed for the different relation). To test your mastery of these three types of signal, do the following exercise.

Exercise 11.3

You will find in the following list four pairs of assertions relating as concession/response. Combine each pair at least three times, using a coordinator, a subordinator, and a movable signal. One of each sort of signal is provided for you here: *nevertheless*, *yet*, and *even though* (although you'll have to figure out which is which). Experiment with subordinating either clause. Experiment with the order of the clauses. And choose for yourself at least *one* additional coordinator, subordinator, and movable signal to use. Be sure, also, that you *punctuate* correctly: at least a semicolon between the assertions signalled by a movable signal; a comma or nothing between clauses signalled by a subordinator. An initial subordinate clause is almost always set off by a comma.

> *1. a.* The sun was shining brightly
>   *b.* The air was cold
> *2. a.* She loved to watch reruns of "The Honeymooners"
>   *b.* Reruns of "The Honeymooners" were on while she was at work
> *3. a.* I had gotten twelve hours sleep the night before
>   *b.* I was too sleepy to concentrate on the lecture
> *4. a.* A ceasefire has been in effect since April
>   *b.* Sporadic fighting continues to occur

One type of cause/effect relationship we discussed in Part I was conditional cause/effect, which translates roughly "if x happens, y happens" or (in the negative) "unless x happens, y will happen." See if you can find this rough translation in the following sentences:

> *a.* If it rains, we'll postpone the match.
> *b.* Provided he remembers, Carl will be at the meeting.
> *c.* Given that she really saw us, we're in trouble.
> *d.* Unless she calls back within the hour, I'll sell it to you.
> *e.* If you don't finish your homework, you can't use the car.

Exercise 11.4

Eight pairs of assertions relating as conditional cause/effect (*if x/y*) appear in the following list. Using a variety of the subordinators provided in the following list, combine each pair of assertions into a subordinate-clause/base-clause sentence. Feel free to vary the position of the subordinate clause, putting it before, inside, or after the base (independent) clause.

Subordinators: *if, whenever, provided [that], as long as, unless, given that, anytime [that],* and *each time [that]*

> *1. a.* You can find the book you borrowed
>   *b.* You'll have to buy a new one

2. *a.* You can find the book you borrowed
   b. You won't have to buy a new one
3. *a.* She gets a few dollars in tips
   b. She deposits them in her savings account
4. *a.* The President does in fact intend to balance the budget
   b. He should begin with military spending
5. *a.* She'll buy the stocks
   b. She hears otherwise from you by 3:00 P.M.
6. *a.* The pain is excruciating
   b. He puts full weight on his right foot
7. *a.* The temperature doesn't drop below twenty-nine degrees
   b. The fruit won't be damaged
8. *a.* The telephone rings
   b. The dog cowers in the corner

In illustrating the subordinate-clause/base-clause structure, we have used the concession/response relation—

> While many animals have communications systems, only human beings can be said to have true language

—and two sorts of cause/effect relation:

> Because AIDS is transmitted through the blood, some persons have developed AIDS after receiving transfusions [regular cause/effect]
>
> *and*
>
> When the plants are put in full sunlight, they develop brown spots on the leaves [conditional cause/effect].

But there are other relations that also use the subordinate-clause/base-clause structure. Two chief ones are the two that in Part I we labeled as location/assertion: one that locates in *time*, one that locates in *space* (or *place*).

Following are two pairs of sentences, one pair using the subordinator *while*, one using the subordinator *when*. In each pair, one is a subordinator of *time*. Which one? And what does the other subordinator signal?

> While Sara washed the car, Molly raked the leaves.
> While I disagree with your position, I admire the way you argue it.
> When it came time to leave, it started to snow.
> When she found her ring, she burst into tears.

The preceding sentences illustrate the fact that subordinators are ambiguous (as are *all* signal words). In the first two sentences, *while* has been used to signal *time* in time/assertion and to signal *concession* in concession/response. In the second two sentences, *when* has been used to signal *time* in time/assertion and to signal an implied *cause* in cause/effect.

In the three sentences that follow, *where* has been used to signal *place, concession,* and *cause.* Be prepared to say which sentence most nearly reflects simple place/assertion, which concession/response, and which cause/effect.

a. Where Jeremy had laid the wet cloth, the finish on the table was ruined.
b. Where once he had been able to carry two-hundred pounds on his shoulders, he now could barely carry the weight of his ancient bones.
c. Where the river turned abruptly to the south, they located their camp.

Exercise 11.5

Following are five subordinators. Using each subordinator twice, write five pairs of subordinate-clause/base-clause sentences. Make the first sentence in each pair either time/assertion or place/assertion; make the second sentence in each pair cause/effect.

| *Examples:* | *(place/assertion)* | Where the creek emptied into the river, a pair of fawns were feeding. |
| | *(cause/effect)* | Where the cat had sharpened her claws, the material was torn. |

Subordinators: *since, as soon as, the time, wherever, everywhere [that]*

Before we leave the subordinate-clause structure, let's look at a few more subordinators and the *x/y* relations they can participate in. Some are subordinators we have already met, serving here a different function.

if	If Thatcher talks tough about communism, she talks even tougher about socialism. (concession/response)
the way	The way she fidgeted, you could sense her anxiety. (evidence/conclusion)
however	However you do it, get it done. (concession/response)
as . . . [so]	As you would have others treat you, you should treat others. (comparison/comparison)
so that	So that he wouldn't forget the tape, he put it by the door. (cause/effect—or, more specifically, goal/action)
whereas	Whereas I can't carry a tune, my sister sings professionally. (contrast/contrast)

until (till)	Until he was forty-eight, his hair was bright red. (time/assertion)
until (till)	Till his attitude improves, he sits on the bench. (conditional cause/effect)
just as	Just as he remembered the question he wanted to ask, the bell rang. (time/assertion)
just as . . . so	Just as there is no life without structure, so there is no life without constraint. (comparison/comparison)

Exercise 11.6

Write ten subordinate-clause/base-clause sentences to illustrate the ten subordinator uses just treated.

Reduced Clauses and Predicate Phrases

Two structures often substitute for the full subordinate clause: the *reduced clause* (sometimes called the *elliptical clause*) and the *predicate phrase*. Both the reduced clause and the predicate phrase come about by deleting redundant information (removing repeated words) —something we've already worked with in coordinate structures.

The reduced clause keeps the subordinator and whatever is not repeated in the base (independent) clause. Compare the two sentences that follow, the first a subordinate-clause/base-clause structure, the second a reduced-clause/base-clause structure:

a. While she ran the final two miles, Frieda began to experience severe stomach cramps.
b. While running the final two miles, Frieda began to experience severe stomach cramps.

Notice that since the same person is the subject of both clauses, the *she* is redundant information. Also since *began* is marked as past tense, *ran* need not be (the signal for past tense is redundant). So *ran* can be changed to a tenseless form—*running*.

But since context can also make the subordinator *while* redundant, we *can* reduce (and sometimes *must* reduce) the reduced clause even further, deleting the subordinator and leaving what is called a *predicate phrase*.

c. Running the final two miles, Frieda began to experience severe stomach cramps.

Notice that such deletion is acceptable *only* when the information is redundant. Why would the following deletions not work?

d. While she ran the final two miles, severe stomach cramps began to plague Frieda.

**e.* While running the final two miles, severe stomach cramps began to plague Frieda.

**f.* Running the final two miles, severe stomach cramps began to plague Frieda.

In edited English sentences *e* and *f* are not acceptable, because *she,* the (deleted) subject of *running,* is not the subject of *began* (that is to say, the subject of the subordinate clause is not the same as the subject of the base clause).

Sometimes the reduced-clause stage sounds strange (as indicated here with an asterisk) and will automatically be reduced to the predicate phrase:

Stanley, because he was hurt and angry, left the room.
*Stanley, because hurt and angry, left the room.
Stanley, hurt and angry, left the room.

Exercise 11.7

Following are twenty subordinate-clause/base-clause sentences. Try reducing the subordinate clauses to reduced clauses and predicate phrases. See if you can find a rule determining which subordinators may or must be deleted (to make the predicate phrase) and which should not (that is, which are needed to signal the relationship). When a sentence has a bracketed word, test both with and without that word. See also which subordinate clauses should not be reduced in any fashion and try to say why they should not.

1. When they were finished with the sanding, they began to apply the stain.

2. When it is thoroughly cooked, you should allow the turkey to cool for at least thirty minutes.

3. Although the tickets were expensive, the members of the entertainment committee voted to buy them [anyway].

4. Since he had left the barrio, Rudy had felt displaced and depressed.

5. If we forget to turn off the headlights, we'll return to a dead battery.

6. Just as it is senseless to die for man-made laws, it is senseless to kill for man-made laws.

7. Although we were exhausted from the walk, we [still] lay awake talking till after midnight.

8. Because he is loud and aggressive, George is unpopular with his classmates.

9. As you were leaving, Marsha said how nice you looked.

10. As she was leaving, Marsha said how nice you looked.

11. Though they were lifelong friends, they rarely saw one another.
12. Even though it was rated R, the movie seemed rather tame.
13. Because she was concerned about her health, she had a medical checkup.
14. Because her parents were concerned about her health, she had a medical checkup.
15. When we found ourselves deeply in debt, we cut up our credit cards.
16. In that Aunt Martha is a believer in family gatherings, Aunt Martha tries to get the family together every Thanksgiving, Christmas, and New Year's Eve.
17. Whenever it is possible, people in sedentary jobs should exercise.
18. Wherever we looked, we saw monarch butterflies.
19. Although he was fiercely proud, Joshua accepted our help gratefully.
20. Although the police were present, several fights broke out in the crowd.

Tenseless Clauses (Nominative Absolutes)

A special structure very much like the subordinate clause is what we'll call the *tenseless clause*. The tenseless clause has no subordinator. And (as its name implies) its verb has no tense. The tenseless clause is a structure we'll find very useful when we explore the includer/included structures. For now let's look at one use it is sometimes put to—to shorten the *cause* clause in a cause/effect relation. In the preceding exercise, sentence 14 allowed no deletion to make a reduced clause or a predicate phrase:

14. Because her parents were deeply concerned about her health, she had a medical checkup.
*Because concerned about her health, she had a medical checkup.
*Concerned about her health, she had a medical checkup. [This last would work if *she* were the subject of "concerned," but it doesn't work for the meaning in sentence 14. The asterisks once again indicate unacceptable structures.]

But there is a structure (though a fairly formal one) that will reduce sentence 14—the structure we're calling the tenseless clause. If we delete the subordinator (*because*) and the auxiliary verb (*were*), we leave a tenseless clause expressing *cause:*

Her parents deeply concerned about her health, she had a medical checkup.

Again, this is a rather formal structure, one you are advised to use sparingly, especially *before* the base clause. (They're more common *after,* particularly in *depictive* writing.) But it's a structure you'll find from time to time in your reading, and there may be occasions in your writing when you'll want to use it. So let's look at the six pairs of sentences that follow and notice how the subordinate clause in the first sentence of each pair becomes a tenseless clause in the second sentence:

1. *a.* Because three feet of snow had fallen during the night, avalanche danger was high.
   b. Three feet of snow having fallen during the night, avalanche danger was high.
2. *a.* In that the state legislature has determined that death by firing squad constitutes cruel and unusual punishment, lethal injections are now to be used in all executions.
   b. The state legislature having determined that death by firing squad constitutes cruel and unusual punishment, lethal injections are now to be used in all executions.
3. *a.* When her piano lessons were over, Debby trudged home.
   b. Her piano lessons over, Debby trudged home.
4. *a.* When their manufacturing costs increased, they raised their prices.
   b. 1. Their manufacturing costs increasing, they raised their prices.
   b. 2. Their manufacturing costs having increased, they raised their prices.
5. *a.* Because his fishing rod was broken, Phil used a willow branch with a piece of line tied to it.
   b. His fishing rod broken, Phil used a willow branch with a piece of line tied to it.
6. *a.* When the meal was finished and the dishes were cleared, we ate our dessert on the patio.
   b. The meal finished and the dishes cleared, we ate our dessert on the patio.

Exercise 11.8

The word *with* is often used to mark a tenseless clause. To practice the feel of tenseless clauses, write out the *b* form of each of the six preceding sentences, starting each with *with.* Then rewrite the following three sentences so that the subordinate clause becomes a tenseless clause. Mark each tenseless clause with *with* or not, as you choose.

1. Because the water pipes were frozen, we couldn't take a shower.
2. When the ambassador had arrived, the orchestra struck up "The Star Spangled Banner."
3. Since Louise has finished law school, her father is planning to retire.

Prepositional Phrases

So far we have looked at four structures of subordination: the subordinate clause, the reduced clause, the predicate phrase, and the tenseless clause. There is a fifth subordinate structure, one that shares many of the functions of the subordinate clause. This fifth structure of subordination is the prepositional phrase. Whereas the subordinate clause consists of a subordinator followed by a base clause—

before the dance had started

—the prepositional phrase consists of a preposition followed by a noun or noun phrase or other nominal—

before breakfast (preposition and noun)

before the dance (preposition and noun phrase)

before dancing with his cousin (preposition and nominal).

Prepositional phrases signal almost all the relations we looked at in Part I. Here are a few illustrations, with the prepositional phrase italicized. Note that the initial prepositional phrase is usually not punctuated, except to prevent misreading. Prepositional phrases placed within or at the end of the main clause are punctuated or not according to a rule we'll look at later.

a. *Unlike his cousin*, Larry doesn't sing. (contrast/contrast)
b. Larry, *unlike his cousin*, doesn't sing. (contrast/contrast)
c. My new brother-in-law swung down from the apple tree *like a gibbon* to meet me. (comparison/comparison)
d. *After dinner* we watched TV. (time/assertion)
e. Her family had gathered *in the living room*. (place/assertion)
f. *Despite the cold* they played outdoors for hours. (contrast/contrast)
g. *For lying under oath*, he was sentenced to thirty days. (cause/effect)
h. *In addition to Frank* there were two other guitarists. (coordinate/coordinate)
i. *According to this dictionary*, the spelling is c-e-m-e-t-e-r-y. (credentials/assertion)

Exercise 11.9

Choosing from the prepositions listed as follows, write at least twenty sentences of your own containing prepositional phrases signalling at least six different relations (cause/effect, concession/response, credentials/assertion, etc.). Be prepared to discuss what relation or relations each preposition might signal. (The following list of prepositions is very long, but there are fully three times that many prepositions to choose from in English.)

Prepositions: *about, above, according to, across, after, against, ahead of, along, among, around, as a consequence of, as compared with, as opposed to, at, back of, because of, before, behind, below, beneath, beside, besides, between, by, by means of, by reason of, concerning, conditional to, contrary to, despite, due to, except for, for, from, in, in addition to, in common with, in comparison to, in contrast with, in lieu of, in place of, in spite of, in support of, in the event of, in view of, including, instead of, into, like, next to, on, onto, opposite, over, past, preliminary to, regardless of, since, thanks to, through, till, under, until, up to, with respect to, with regard to, with the exception of, without, without regard to.*

Cause/Effect *Which* Clause

Another structure of subordination (the sixth) is a structure usually identified only as a relative clause. But it is a special sort of relative clause, one we'll call the "cause/effect *which* clause." Later (in the section "Structures of Expansion") we will look at several other sorts of relative clauses.

Relative clauses resemble subordinate clauses in that both have all the elements of a full sentence: a subject and a tense-marked predicate. But whereas the subordinate clause *adds* a subordinator to an already complete base clause—

the dog was ill + because = because the dog was ill

—the relative clause *substitutes* a relative word (*which* in the case we're looking at here) for a word in the original base clause:

It made him late + which = which made him late.

Like subordinate clauses, relative clauses are *dependent* elements and usually are not punctuated as complete sentences. The relative clause we are looking at here, the cause/effect *which* clause, *always* follows (though not necessarily immediately) a full base clause, from which it is normally separated by a comma, dash, or parenthesis. Following are two full base clauses, separated by a period. By substituting *which* for a word in the second base clause, we can create a cause/effect *which* clause and make the two base clauses into a single sentence:

> He raised his head quickly. This made him feel dizzy.

> He raised his head quickly, which made him feel dizzy.
> *or*
> He raised his head quickly—which made him feel dizzy.
> *or*
> He raised his head quickly (which made him feel dizzy).

We've called this the cause/effect *which* clause because it always names an effect for which the base clause is the cause. But we wouldn't name it at all unless there were at least one other type of *which* clause. And indeed there is—one we will look at in the next section, "Structures of Expansion." Because it is easy to confuse the two types, teachers often warn students against using the cause/effect *which* clause at all. Below is a sentence that leaves the reader confused as to which type of *which* clause is intended:

> On the back porch she found a basket of kittens, which struck her as odd.

The ambiguity of the last sentence stems from the fact that *which* can refer to *kittens* (the kittens struck her as odd; they were odd little kittens), to *basket of kittens* (the basket of kittens struck her as odd; it was a strange basket of kittens), or to the entire sentence *on the back porch she found a basket of kittens* (the *fact* that there was a basket of kittens on her back porch struck her as odd). To prevent this ambiguity, you should avoid using the cause/effect *which* clause unless it is clear that *which* refers to *the entire preceding assertion*, that the *which* clause names an effect for which the preceding assertion is the cause. The last sentence should have been left as two:

> On the back porch she found a basket of kittens. This fact struck her as odd.

Exercise 11.10

The following are eight pairs of base clauses. Each pair can be made into a single sentence by making a cause/effect *which* clause of the second base clause. But some of the resulting *which* clauses will be ambiguous. Where you discover such ambiguity, copy the two base clauses as they are here—two full sentences separated by a period. Be prepared to discuss the ambiguity.

1. One of the jurors refused to be persuaded by other eleven. This resulted in a hung jury.
2. The library was closed. This meant we'd have to find another place to study.
3. He had lost his twelve-year-old German shepherd. This left him without a companion.
4. They had supported their case with data from a single source. He said this was wrong.
5. They are leading by sixteen points with less than two minutes to go. This virtually assures them the victory.
6. She spent the evening working on the painting. This gave her great pleasure.
7. She broke the engagement after three weeks. They said this left him devastated.
8. Darren graduated from Harvard. This made him proud.

Includer/Included Subordination

The last structures of subordination we'll look at for a while are those of the includer/included relation. Subordinate structures of the includer/included relation are basically deletion structures. Subordination is signalled by the deletion structures themselves, by the punctuation, and by the logical relation (often including a signal word). Let's see how these three signals work by combining two assertions:

a. Jason was fascinated by everything in the pet store
b. Jason was fascinated by the tropical fish } particularly

- Jason was fascinated by everything in the pet store, particularly the tropical fish.

First, the deletion structure itself: Everything in *b* is redundant except the phrase "the tropical fish," clearly a subordinate (dependent) structure. Second, the comma preceding the deletion structure signals that what follows is subordinate to the base clause (and we'll see in a moment that three other punctuation marks could be used to signal this subordination). Third, the logical relation between "everything in the pet store" and "the tropical fish" is obviously one where the first term *logically includes* the second term (where, in other words, the phrase "the tropical fish" is logically subordinate to "everything in the pet store"). This logical relation is specified by the signal word "particularly."

As mentioned before, there are four punctuation marks to signal subordination when the included (subordinate) element *follows* a completed base clause:

1. Jason was fascinated by everything in the pet store, particularly the tropical fish.
2. Jason was fascinated by everything in the pet store—particularly the tropical fish.
3. Jason was fascinated by everything in the pet store: particularly the tropical fish.
4. Jason was fascinated by everything in the pet store (particularly the tropical fish).

These four ways are not totally interchangeable, as we will see in a moment. For one thing, the comma is not always an alternative if what follows also contains commas. For another, the colon is a fairly formal mark and is most common as a signal for the *x namely y* relation. But all of these marks are in fact legitimate ways of ending a base clause that contains an includer term and of introducing the subordinate (included) term.

Exercise 11.11

Following are eleven pairs of assertions relating as includer/included. Combine them four times each in the fashion just shown, with the base clause (containing the includer term) followed by each choice of punctuation mark in turn. Use the signal word or not as you feel is appropriate. Also, feel free to substitute an equivalent signal word for the one provided.

Example:　He found what he'd been looking for since 8:00 A.M. ⎱
　　　　　 He found his contact lens　　　　　　　　　　　 ⎰ namely

He found what he'd been looking for since 8:00 A.M.,namely, his contact lens.
He found what he'd been looking for since 8:00 A.M.—his contact lens.
He found what he'd been looking for since 8:00 A.M.: his contact lens.
He found what he'd been looking for since 8:00 A.M. (his contact lens).

1. *a.* There were enough tacos for everyone ⎱
　 b. There were enough tacos for "twelve-taco" Tommy ⎰ including

2. *a.* Each day you should eat at least one piece of citrus fruit ⎱
　 b. Each day you should eat at least a grapefruit ⎰ for example

3. *a.* We bought their latest album ⎱
　 b. We bought "Getting Sick" ⎰ namely

4. *a.* This economic trend hurts almost everyone ⎱
　 b. This economic trend hurts the farmers ⎰ particularly

5. *a.* Be sure to pack something warm to wear ⎫
   b. Be sure to pack a sweater ⎬ such as

6. *a.* Morris won fourth prize in the contest ⎫
   b. Morris won a two-week vacation for two in Acapulco ⎬ namely

7. *a.* That term I got an *A* in every subject ⎫
   b. That term I got an *A* in organic chemistry ⎬ including

8. *a.* Her shoulder hurts all the time ⎫
   b. Her shoulder hurts when she tries to lift anything ⎬ particularly

9. *a.* On the table lay the letter he had been dreading ⎫
   b. On the table lay the premium notice for his car insurance ⎬ namely

10. *a.* On the table lay the premium notice for his car insurance ⎫
    b. On the table lay the letter he had been dreading ⎬ [nothing]

11. *a.* They had stolen everything ⎫
    b. They had stolen the $1,700 burglar-alarm system ⎬ including

Exercise 11.12

In the previous exercise the included elements were all added after the includer clause was grammatically complete (which is the most common way in professional writing). But the included element can also come *before* or *within* the includer clause.

When the included element comes before the includer clause, it will normally be set off by a comma: "His hair matted, Justin came to the front door." (We'll practice this option in Exercise 11.15.)

When the included element comes *within* the includer clause (*interrupts* the includer clause), it is normally set off by a *pair* of marks: a pair of commas, dashes, or parentheses.

In this exercise you will be deleting redundant information and placing the included element *within* the includer clause, immediately after the includer term. You will set off *both* ends of the included element, using the *same mark* at each end (though you should vary the pair of marks from sentence to sentence till you've tried all the options). With some sentences you will be including more than one element.

Example: *a.* The dogs had treed a raccoon ⎫
            b. One dog was a terrier ⎬ and ⎬ namely
            c. One dog was a cocker spaniel ⎭

The dogs, a terrier and a cocker spaniel, had treed a raccoon.
or
The dogs—a terrier and a cocker spaniel—had treed a raccoon.
or
The dogs (a terrier and a cocker spaniel) had treed a raccoon.

1. *a.* The car was upside down in the ditch } namely
   b. The car was a late-model Porsche }

2. *a.* His luggage had not been put on the plane } namely
   b. His luggage was two suitcases } and
   c. His luggage was a box of books }

3. *a.* The economies of many Middle-Eastern countries are dominated by the oil market
   b. The economy of Iran is dominated by the oil market } particularly
   c. The economy of Iraq is dominated by the oil market } and
   d. The economy of The United Arab Emirates is dominated by the oil market.

4. *a.* Some bivalve mollusks can swim by snapping their shells together rapidly } for example
   b. Certain clams can swim by snapping their shells together rapidly } and
   c. Scallops can swim by snapping their shells together rapidly }

5. *a.* Stanford and Bernice had been seen walking on the beach } including
   b. Stanford was in U.S. Army fatigues } and
   c. Bernice was in shorts } and
   d. Bernice was in a halter top }
   e. Bernice was in a broad-brimmed straw hat }

In the two previous exercises the focus was on the whole/part relationship (everyone/"twelve-taco" Tommy) and the general/specific relationship (something warm to wear/a sweater). The following exercises concentrate on the operation/phase and operation/stage relationships. This is because these two "operation" relationships require slightly different punctuation (the colon is almost never used, and the comma can be used even if what follows contains commas) and involve a special sort of deletion. Here is a model for what we'll be doing in the next exercise.

a. The car sped around the corner } operation/stage
b. The car skidded as it hit the patch of gravel } or phase

● The car sped around the corner, skidding as it hit the patch of gravel

or

● The car sped around the corner—skidding as it hit the patch of gravel.

Two things to note in our model: (1) only two marks of punctuation are normally used to separate the main-clause *operation* from its subordinate-phrase *stage* or *phase*—the comma or the dash; (2) the original verb *skidded* becomes *skidding* in the modifier (this is what we'll call *deletion of tense*.)

Note the difference between these two ways of combining the same two assertions:

The car sped around the corner
The car skidded as it hit the patch of gravel } and

a. The car sped around the corner and skidded as it hit the patch of gravel.

The car sped around the corner
The car skidded as it hit the patch of gravel } operation/stage

b. The car sped around the corner, skidding as it hit the patch of gravel.

In the *a* version both verbs are marked as past tense (the car *sped* and *skidded*). This marks them as coordinate, which means that we'll read the *a* version to say that *first* the car sped around the corner and *then* (after it had rounded the corner) it skidded on the gravel.

In the *b* version, only the verb *sped* is marked for tense; the other verb (*skidding*) has had the tense removed. This allows us to understand the *b* version to mean that *sped around the corner* names the operation and *skidding as it hit the patch of gravel* names a stage or phase of that operation, a little event that takes place *within* the larger event.

Exercise 11.13

The following six pairs of sentences relate as operation/stage. Combine the pairs of sentences into ten main-clause/subordinate-phrase sentences, deleting redundancies, including the tense in the second assertion (by changing the verb to *-ing*) and separating the main clause and subordinate phrase with a comma or a dash. Add the included element after the main clause.

Examples: He swung the bat
He snapped his wrists at the last second } operation/stage

● He swung the bat, snapping his wrists at the last second.

   1. a. He turned off the television
      b. He hit the switch with the heel of his hand } operation/stage

2. *a.* They walked through the park
   b. They scuffed their feet through the dry leaves } operation/stage

3. *a.* I took the aspirin
   b. I downed the full glass of water in one breath } operation/stage

4. *a.* The president strode to the podium
   b. The president straightened his tie with his left hand } operation/stage or phase

5. *a.* The storm raged for days
   b. The storm slammed the coast of Louisiana on the morning of 28 August } operation/stage

6. *a.* She uncovered the fragile jawbone methodically
   b. She chipped away the encrusted rock with a dental pick } operation/stage

In the exercise you just completed, the subject of the operation clause was the subject of the stage clause also, which allowed it to be deleted as redundant information:

He swung the bat
He snapped his wrists at the last second } operation/stage

● He swung the bat, snapping his wrists at the last second.

This is typical of the operation/stage relationship. But with two other includer/included relations—operation/phase and whole/part—it is typical to name a new subject (a part of the whole) in the included clause:

a. The child answered the principal's questions
b. Her voice trembled as she spoke } operation/phase

a. He lay on his back in the sun
b. Beads of sweat glistened on his forehead } whole/part

So when we delete the redundant information this time, the subject of the *b* clause will have to remain. Only the tense of the verb is redundant. The resulting subordinate structure is one you'll remember as a tenseless clause:

The child answered the principal's questions, *her voice trembling as she spoke.*
He lay on his back in the sun, *beads of sweat glistening on his forehead.*

Exercise 11.14

The following are six pairs of base clauses, relating as operation/phase or whole/part. In each pair the *b* clause has its own subject, a part of the whole named in the *a* clause. In making the *b* clause subordinate (a tenseless clause), you will be deleting only tense. In this exercise, deleting tense will involve either deleting the tense-marked form of *be* (*is, are, was*, or *were*) or changing the verb to an *-ing* form. Add the included element after the main clause.

Examples:

    a. Donna walked down the sidewalk
    b. The tip of her white cane swung smoothly from side to side   } operation/phase

- Donna walked down the sidewalk, the tip of her white cane swinging smoothly from side to side.

    a. The kitten crouched in the back of the cage
    b. His ears were flat against his head   } whole/part

- The kitten crouched in the back of the cage, his ears flat against his head.

  1. *a.* The fish rested on the reef
      b. Its gills pulsed rhythmically
  2. *a.* A single red rose drooped in the vase
      b. The edges of its petals were nearly black
  3. *a.* He threw back his head and shouted
      b. His voice boomed through the cathedral
  4. *a.* The cat crossed the room slowly
      b. His tail twitched with every step
  5. *a.* The rice boiled on the back burner
      b. The lid of the pan tapped metallically as the steam escaped
  6. *a.* Denise was still sitting in the waiting room
      b. Her hands were folded on her lap

In depictive writing, where these *included* subordinate elements are most often found, they usually appear *after* the base clause, the way they have appeared in most of the last several exercises. But they can also appear *before* the base clause or *within* the base clause.

Exercise 11.15

Following are the same six pairs of base clauses from Exercise 11.14. Combine them twice each, putting the subordinate phrase *before* the main clause the first time (set off by a comma) and *within* the main clause the second time (set off on *both* sides by a *pair* of marks—either two commas, two dashes, or two parentheses). Not every subordinate phrase will sound natural or totally logical in the initial or medial position. Be prepared to discuss (1) which results sound unnatural and (2) why they do. Note any changes in meaning.

Examples: *a.* The child answered the principal's questions
b. Her voice trembled as she spoke

- Her voice trembling as she spoke, the child answered the principal's questions.

or

- The child—her voice trembling as she spoke—answered the principal's questions.

a. He opened the box
b. His eyes were eager

- His eyes eager, he opened the box.

or

- He, his eyes eager, opened the box.

1. a. The fish rested on the reef
  b. Its gills pulsed rhythmically
2. a. A single red rose drooped in the vase
  b. The edges of the petals were nearly black
3. a. He threw back his head and shouted
  b. His voice boomed through the cathedral
4. a. The cat crossed the room slowly
  b. His tail twitched with every step
5. a. The rice boiled on the back burner
  b. The lid of the pan tapped metallically as the steam escaped
6. a. Denise was still sitting in the waiting room
  b. Her hands were folded on her lap

Exercise 11.16

The same pairs of base clauses as appeared in the two previous exercises are used again here. This time, though, additional clauses have been added—some coordinate to the *b* clause, some not. Experiment with incorporating these additional clauses. Be prepared to explain why you incorporated the new clauses as you did. (The clauses won't necessarily end up in the same order they're given in here. Your reasons for placing them where you did will be important.)

In this exercise you will be making more complicated punctuation choices. But the rules you learned for setting off subordinate units from the base clause apply also to setting them off from other subordinate units: set off *any* unit from the unit it is subordinate to; if it interrupts (comes within) the unit it is subordinate to, set it off with a pair of marks, one on each end. Remember that the marks that work in pairs are parentheses, dashes, and commas.

Examples:

    a. The child answered the principal's questions
    b. Her voice trembled as she spoke
    c. The child was near tears
    d. Her chin quivered as she spoke

- The child, near tears, answered the principal's questions, her voice trembling and her chin quivering as she spoke.

    a. He lay on his back in the sun
    b. Beads of sweat glistened on his forehead
    c. He was pale from the long winter
    d. Beads of sweat glistened on his upper lip

- Pale from the long winter, he lay on his back in the sun, beads of sweat glistening on his forehead and upper lip.

1. *a.* The fish rested on the reef
    b. Its gills pulsed rhythmically
    c. Its bulging eyes rolled as it scanned the scene
2. *a.* A single red rose drooped in the vase
    b. The edges of its petals were nearly black
    c. Its stem was a limp, green arc
3. *a.* He threw back his head and shouted
    b. His voice boomed through the cathedral
    c. His long hair was splayed out over his shoulders
    d. His voice echoed through the long, empty halls
4. *a.* The cat crossed the room slowly
    b. His tail twitched with every step
    c. The cat cast furtive glances at the guests
    d. The white tip of his tail flicked sharply
    e. The cat disappeared into the darkened hallway
5. *a.* The rice boiled on the back burner
    b. The lid of the pan tapped metallically as the steam escaped
    c. The sound was as steady as a metronome
    d. The steam filled the room with a warm, starchy aroma
6. *a.* Denise was still sitting in the waiting room
    b. Her hands were folded on her lap
    c. Denise was apparently studying the wallpaper
    d. Denise was apparently tracing the monotonous pattern with unblinking eyes
    e. The pattern was alternating green and grey stripes
    f. Her left foot tapped idly

Exercise 11.17

Option 2 of Essay Assignment Two (from Part II) required you to describe a static scene, concentrating on parts (and subparts), qualities, and comparisons. You are to repeat that exercise (choosing a new topic or redoing the old one, even working with your original sentences), but this time the goal is to end up with a single sentence, with only one independent (base) clause.

The assignment has been modeled for you below. The first (*A*) description contains twenty-eight base clauses. The second (*B*) description (the model for this assignment) contains only one base clause (italicized to help you identify it). The *B* description is shorter by sixty-seven words, yet it contains essentially the same *information* as *A*. Note what deletions have been made to shorten version number two. Note also the punctuation in the second version, especially the use of the colon, the semicolons, and the marks setting off elements *within* elements. Be prepared to discuss the questions at the end.

Description A

He entered the greenhouse. The humid air briefly fogged his glasses. The humid air briefly suppressed his breathing. He surveyed the damage.

A tray of squash seedlings had been overturned. Many of the uprooted seedlings lay scattered across the floor. Bits of potting mixture clung to their roots. Their paired leaves were beginning to curl. Their paired leaves were thick green lobes. All this was just to the left of the door.

The large clay pot with his prized aloe vera plant had been smashed on the concrete walkway. The whole thing looked like an enormous ruined blossom. The plant was in the center. It was a flattened pinwheel of thick, green-mottled leaves. The leaves were like swords. Some of the leaves were broken. They oozed a fluid. The fluid was viscous and slimy. A black disk of rich loam earth surrounded the plant. Shards of broken pottery surrounded the disk. The shards were like brittle petals. All this was on the concrete walkway in front of him.

And liquid fertilizer and pesticide had been spattered everywhere. Irregular circles of dark-brown fluid stained the clear-plastic walls. Rivulets of dark-brown fluid stained the clear-plastic walls. The sharp chemical odor filled the steamy room. The sharp chemical odor burned his nose. The sharp chemical odor burned his eyes.

Description B

He entered the greenhouse, the humid air briefly fogging his glasses and suppressing his breathing, *and surveyed the damage*: just to the left of the door an overturned tray of squash seedlings, many scattered across the floor—bits of potting mixture clinging to their roots—their paired leaves, thick green lobes, beginning to curl; on the concrete walkway in front of him the large clay pot with his prized aloe vera plant, smashed, the whole like an enormous ruined blossom—the plant in the center, a flattened pinwheel of thick, green-mottled, sword-like leaves, some broken, oozing a viscous, slimy fluid, surrounding the plant a black disk of rich loam earth, surrounding the disk shards of broken pottery, like brittle petals; and everywhere liquid fertilizer and pesticide splattered, circles and rivulets of dark-brown fluid staining the clear-plastic walls, the sharp chemical odor filling the steamy room, burning his nose and eyes.

First, let's recognize that, outside this assignment, you may choose not to write as long a sentence as the *B* version. Perhaps this will be a one-shot tour de force for you. But if you can do this assignment with skill, you at least know what you're capable of.

Second, let's recognize that, long as the *B* version is, it is shorter, by almost a third, than the *A* version, the same information expressed as twenty-eight separate base clauses. And in some ways (particularly in terms of placement options—putting structures *inside* structures), the *B* version is clearer and easier to read.

Consider these questions for discussion.

1. What does the use of the colon and semicolons enable us to signal about the chunking in the *B* version?
2. What options in placement does the *B* version give us that the *A* version doesn't? Specifically deal with the place/assertion relation and with the issue of relating (as whole/part, whole/quality, etc.) three or more elements in the same base clause.
3. What has been done to remove tense from the subordinate structures?

❖━━━━━━━━━━━━━━━━━━━━━━━━━━━━━━━❖

Essay Assignment Seven
Using Structures of Subordination

Essay Assignment Three (from part II) required that you depict an activity, concentrating on stages, phases, qualities (manner), and comparisons. You are to repeat that assignment (choosing a new subject or redoing the old subject, even working with your original sentences if you wish); but this time, by using subordinate structures, you are to further expand your subject, expressing more information in fewer words and sentences than in your original effort. Try at least one or two fairly ambitious sentences (fifty words, say), in which you have managed to include a series, with modifiers for each item in the series and with modifiers of some of the modifiers—in much the same fashion as the *B* version in the previous exercise.

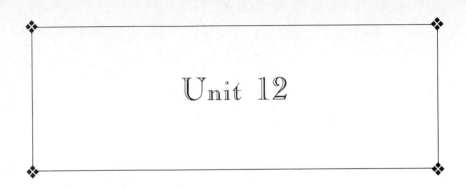

Structures of Expansion

Introduction

The last structures we'll look at are those we'll call structures of expansion. To understand what is meant by the term "structures of expansion," one must be able to see certain similarities and certain differences. For example, one must be able to see sentences *a* and *b* as saying essentially the same thing:

a. That guy loves that student.
b. That red-headed Irish guy I introduced you to at Jeanne's party last week really loves that little exchange student from Poland.

And one must be able to see sentences *c* and *d* as saying essentially different things:

c. I gave that box of toys to my neighbor who has six kids.
d. I gave that box of toys to my neighbor, who has six kids.

We'll leave the difference between *c* and *d* for later; for now let's see just what sorts of structures we're expanding in our "structures of expansion."

The easiest way to see is to take another look at the base clause, this time focusing on six basic *structural patterns* the base clause can take. In doing this, we'll be using some time-honored grammatical terms—terms your teacher may very well ask you to learn. And as an educated person you yourself should want to know these terms. But if learning grammatical terminology has always been difficult for you, I ask you—before you despair—to consider these three facts: (1) if you can read this book, you already know all the grammatical *structures* we'll look at, whether or not you can learn their names; (2) you'll be able to do all the exercises in this section, whether or not you learn the terminology; and (3) the approach used here is pretty simple, so this time you just might learn the grammatical terms after all!

First, here is a quick definition of a term we've already used, *base clause*, a structure also often referred to as *main clause* or *independent clause*. A normal base clause is a two-stage operation, the first stage of which is called the *subject*, the second the *predicate*. Here are twelve base clauses, divided (by a slash) between the subject and the predicate.

1. Springsteen/sang.
2. The singer many people call "The Boss"/sang for several hours in a concert for which the tickets sold out in record time.
3. That/is untrue.
4. What you just said/is as untrue as anything I have ever heard in all my days on earth.
5. She/became his partner.
6. The shy Navajo girl from the isolated reservation in northern Arizona/became his partner in one of the most successful educational enterprises of the decade.
7. The wedding/would be that month.
8. The wedding that all Ambrosia had been waiting breathlessly for months to hear announced/would be the very month that Prince Harland returned from his pilgrimage to Lambrustina.
9. It/causes problems.
10. Trying to devote adequate attention to both your career and your love life/often causes such problems as few people are able to cope with.
11. We/told them that.
12. Those of us who had arrived by 6:00 P.M./told whoever came late what the chairman had said.

Exercise 12.1

The following are twelve base clauses, similar to the ones you just looked at. Copy them on a separate sheet of paper, putting a slash (/) between the subject and the predicate. (Please note that in edited writing *no* mark of punctuation is used to signal the juncture between subject and predicate. Whenever a mark of punctuation appears at the juncture between subject and predicate, it is one of a *pair* of marks setting off a *modifier* coming between subject and predicate.)

1. The dog was barking.
2. The little cocker-spaniel dog that my cousin received for her birthday was still barking when I returned from the post office.
3. Mr. Kauffman was friendly.
4. The lively septuagenarian immigrant who owned the candy store below the flat where I grew up was always friendly to the children in the neighborhood.
5. She remained an ally.
6. The elderly widow whose house we had painted as a scouting project remained an ally when we got in trouble with the police that summer.
7. The car was outside.
8. The Italian sports car that both Diedre and Simone had claimed to have seen at the restaurant earlier that evening was outside in the parking lot when the dance broke up.
9. They did their homework.
10. All the members of the fraternity who were on academic probation did their homework each night under the supervision of the academic chairman himself.
11. She made him a cheesecake.
12. The girl my older brother has been dating these last six months made my younger brother a strawberry cheesecake in return for the work he did on her car.

Basic Sentence Patterns

In the previous exercise (as in the set of twelve base clauses we looked at earlier—as you probably noticed) the sentences were paired, each odd-numbered sentence representing a "bare-bones" structure and the even-numbered sentence following it representing an *expansion* of that structure:

The car was outside.
The Italian sports car that both Diedre and Simone had claimed
    to have seen at the restaurant earlier that evening was outside in
    the parking lot when the dance broke up.

In addition, each pair represents a certain *type* of structure—what might be called a *basic sentence pattern*. Another way of saying it is that all the sentences in the English language are variations on these six sentence patterns. It's time to take a closer look at these patterns and at the three basic ways in which these patterns are expanded. Again, this discussion will involve some grammatical terminology. But it's less important that you become completely comfortable with the terminology than that you become comfortable expanding the patterns represented here. In the following list are those six patterns, with a representative sentence illustrating each:

1. She slept [soundly]: subject/intransitive verb [+optional adverbial element]
2. She seemed angry: subject/linking verb + adjective complement
3. She became chairperson: subject/linking verb + noun complement
4. She is here: subject/linking verb + adverbial complement
5. She baked bread: subject/transitive verb + direct object
6. She told me something: subject/ditransitive verb + indirect object + direct object

All six of these patterns have a subject slot and a predicate slot. And since any noun or nounlike structure can occupy the subject slot, the differences separating the six patterns lie in the predicate. Here, briefly, are the points that differentiate the six sentence patterns.

Pattern 1: She slept [soundly].

The predicate slot in pattern 1 sentences has what is called an intransitive verb—a verb without an object or a complement but a verb that may have an adverbial element. What this means is that a pattern 1 sentence will have a subject doing something (and perhaps doing it in a certain manner or at a certain time or place, etc.—adverbial issues), but there will be nothing answering what or who receives the action of the verb. Notice that in the following sentences there is either *nothing* accompanying the (intransitive) verb or that what accompanies the verb answers adverbial questions (*how, why, where, when*, etc.), not the questions *what* or *whom*:

John smoked. [nothing]
John smoked furiously. (how)
John smoked because he was nervous. (why)
John smoked after dinner. (when)
John smoked despite the risk. (*even though x*)

All these are pattern 1 sentences. If we add a unit that answers *what* John smoked, we change to pattern 5:

John smoked nervously. (pattern 1)
John smoked the cigar nervously. (pattern 5)

Exercise 12.2

Six pairs of sentences follow. One sentence in each pair is a pattern 1; the other is not. Determine which member of the pair is a pattern 1 sentence.

1. a. Sara moved cautiously.
   b. Sara moved the end table.
2. a. He sang two German folk songs.
   b. He sang with great enthusiasm.
3. a. My dad walked to the drugstore to get a newspaper.
   b. My dad walked old Tyrone around the block.
4. a. The professor nodded encouragingly.
   b. The professor nodded her head.
5. a. The team flew kites for kicks.
   b. The team flew to Denver for the finals.
6. a. Marvella left through the back door while I was on the phone.
   b. Marvella left many questions unanswered.

Pattern 2: She seemed angry.

Pattern 1 sentences have an intransitive verb. That verb may or may not have one or more adverbial modifiers:

She slept.
She slept soundly.
She slept soundly in the big bed.
She slept soundly in the big bed until 9:30 the next morning.

Pattern 2 sentences (and pattern 3 and 4 sentences also) have an intransitive verb too, but it's an intransitive verb of a special kind, called a *linking verb*: it always requires a *completing* unit, a *complement*, as they're traditionally called. *She slept* is a complete sentence; the added elements are optional. *She seemed* is not a complete sentence; it needs a *completer*, a *complement*. In the case of pattern 2 sentences, the completer is an adjective or adjectival unit, with or without its own modifiers:

a. She seemed angry.
b. She seemed particularly bright.

c. She seemed pleased with the result.

d. The milk tasted sour.

e. The bath felt rather hot.

f. It was beautiful.

g. He looked confused.

h. They became friendlier.

i. The room fell quiet.

j. The baby grew fussy.

k. Dwight remained totally unconscious.

l. That would be fine.

m. Learning the rules wasn't easy.

Exercise 12.3

Following are ten pairs of sentences. One sentence in each pair is a pattern 2, the other is not. Determine which member of the pair is a pattern 2 sentence—that is, which has a linking verb followed by an adjective or adjectival complement.

1. a. He felt the material of the jacket.
   b. He felt sick at his stomach.
2. a. Maria became our sponsor.
   b. Maria became quite agitated.
3. a. We stayed warm.
   b. We stayed after.
4. a. The bird appeared injured.
   b. The bird appeared at the window.
5. a. His arm went limp.
   b. His arm went around her waist.
6. a. Her neighbor grew roses.
   b. Her cheeks grew rosy.
7. a. Sandy remained after the meeting.
   b. Sandy remained affable to a degree.
8. a. Those sweaters run slightly large.
   b. The colors of those sweaters run sometimes.
9. a. We got down from the dais.
   b. We got sick from the shrimp.
10. a. He appeared at a loss for words.
    b. He appeared at a benefit for orphans.

Pattern 3: She became chairperson.

Like pattern 2 sentences, the pattern 3 sentence has a linking verb followed by a complement. But whereas the complement in pattern 2 is an *adjective, describing* the subject, the complement in pattern 3 is a *noun, renaming* or categorizing the subject:

Pattern 2: Louisa is friendly.
Pattern 3: Louisa is my friend.

Note that in the preceding pattern 3 sentence the terms *Louisa* and *my friend* refer to the same individual.

As we have seen, many verbs can serve as the linking verb in a pattern 2 sentence: *be, get, grow, seem, become, feel, taste, look, appear,* and so on. But just three verbs account for almost all the pattern 3 sentences we meet: *be* (*is, are, was,* etc.), *become,* and *remain.*

a. He is a good student.
b. She was my girlfriend in grade school.
c. I am your friend.
d. They are hardworking women.
e. We were the first people in line.
f. He has been many things.
g. This will be my first time.
h. She became a nuisance.
i. This remains our biggest obstacle.

Still, there are a few others, particularly in British English. (In American English these others sometimes combine with *to be*.)

j. He grew [to be] a fine young man.
k. She seems [to be] a good risk.
l. Donald really looks the part.
m. We stayed friends.
n. This appears [to be] a viable alternative.

Exercise 12.4

Six pairs of sentences follow. One sentence in each pair is pattern 3; the other is not. Determine which member of the pair is pattern 3—that is, which member has a linking verb followed by a noun or nominal renaming or categorizing the subject.

1. a. The taxes became a burden.
   b. The taxes became burdensome.
2. a. Whitney remained behind.
   b. Whitney remained vice-president.
3. a. We were all tired.
   b. We were all experienced sailors.
4. a. My uncle acted foolish.
   b. My uncle acted the fool.
5. a. I felt the center of the wheel.
   b. I felt the center of attention.

6. *a*. They were people we all admired.
   b. They were on the patio with people we all admired.

Pattern 4: She is here.

Pattern 2 sentences have a linking verb and an adjective complement. Pattern 3 sentences have a linking verb and a noun complement. Pattern 4 sentences have a linking verb and an *adverbial* complement.

You'll recall that pattern 1 sentences could also have an adverbial element following the verb:

He cried [pitifully].

The difference between patterns 1 and 4 is that in pattern 1 the sentence feels complete without the adverb—

He cried

—but in pattern 4 the adverb complement is needed to complete the sentence:

He was outside.

Only two verbs account for essentially all the pattern 4 sentences: *be* and *get*. And the adverb complements are all adverbs of time or place. *Be* uses both; *get* uses only adverbs of place.

a. He was in the basement.
b. She will be there.
c. The party was after the dance.
d. The party was in the recreation room.
e. She got to France.
f. The thermometer got to ninety degrees.

Exercise 12.5

Following are four pairs of sentences. One sentence in each pair is a pattern 4; the other is not. Determine which member of the pair is pattern 4—that is, which member has a linking verb followed by an adverbial of time or place.

1. a. Lana was outraged.
   b. Lana was outside.
2. a. The party will be later.
   b. The party will be expensive.

> 3. *a.* We got as far as page 67.
>   *b.* We got a package in the mail.
> 4. *a.* Miller was down in the dumps.
>   *b.* Miller was down in the dump.

Pattern 5: *She baked bread.*

The majority of the sentences you will read and write are pattern 5 sentences: subject, transitive verb, and direct object. One thing that distinguishes the linking verb plus noun complement (*She became chairperson*—pattern 3) from transitive verb plus object (*She baked bread*—pattern 5) is that in pattern 3 the subject and the complement are the same (*she* and *chairperson* refer to the same individual), while in pattern 5 the subject and the object are different.* Another characteristic of pattern 5 sentences is that they usually can be made passive:

She baked the bread (active)

The bread was baked [by her] (passive).

Only a transitive (pattern 5) or ditransitive (pattern 6) verb can normally be made passive.

> * The exception to this general rule are the so-called reflexive (-self) pronouns: *She hurt herself* is pattern 5, even though *she* and *herself* refer to the same person.

Exercise 12.6

Six pairs of sentences follow. One sentence in each pair is a pattern 5; the other is not. Determine which member of each pair is a pattern 5 sentence. Then, on a separate sheet of paper, write out that sentence as a passive one (making the direct object the new subject and either deleting the original subject or including it in a *by* prepositional phrase).

Example:
    a. Barry remained my closest friend.
    b. Barry insulted my closest friend.

- My closest friend was insulted.
  or
- My closest friend was insulted by Barry.

> 1. *a.* The graduating class honored Mr. Neiman.
>   *b.* The graduating class cheered when Mr. Neiman stood.
> 2. *a.* Stan related the facts of the case.
>   *b.* Stan related well with others.
> 3. *a.* We gathered in the basement.
>   *b.* We cleaned the basement.

4. *a*. The children swept the sidewalks.
   b. The children swept past us.
5. *a*. Cynthia drank the rest of the lemonade.
   b. Cynthia is the one who drank the lemonade.
6. *a*. The movers arrived in a twenty-eight-foot van.
   b. The movers broke a very expensive vase.

Pattern 6: *She told me something.*

Our final pattern is one with a special sort of transitive verb (often called a "ditransitive" verb), with two objects: an *indirect object* and a *direct object*. Sometimes the indirect object *precedes* the direct object.

We told them the truth.
Sara bought Dan a book.
Drew asked Laura a question.
He gave the menu a glance.

Sometimes the indirect object *follows* the direct object, in which case it will be preceded by the preposition *to* or *for* (or occasionally *at* or *of*).

We told the truth to them.
Sara bought a book for Dan.
Drew asked a question of Laura.
He gave a glance at the menu.

Exercise 12.7

Following are six pairs of sentences. One sentence in each pair is a pattern 6; the other is not. Determine which sentence in each pair is a pattern 6 sentence (that is to say, which one has a ditransitive verb followed by an indirect object and direct object). Then, on a separate piece of paper, rewrite the patten 6 sentence so that the indirect object (preceded by *to*, *for*, *at*, or *of*) comes *after* the direct object.

Example: *a*. She wrote a note on the blackboard.
              b. She wrote him a note.

● She wrote a note to him.

1. *a*. Martha fried me two eggs.
   b. Martha lay in the sun after work.
2. *a*. The lead climber dropped Calvin a rope.
   b. The lead climber dropped twenty feet to the ledge.
3. *a*. The mayor spoke persuasively about the new library.
   b. The mayor sent my parents an invitation.

4. *a.* Stan and Martha threw a party when they got their tax return.
   b. Stan threw Martha a warning glance.
5. *a.* Someone left me instructions.
   b. Someone left as I was coming in.
6. *a.* We wrote essays in our English composition class.
   b. We wrote the police an account of the fight.

Exercise 12.8

Pattern 6 sentences, like pattern 5 sentences, can be made passive. Either the indirect object or the direct object can become the subject of the passive verb. Whichever one does not become the subject remains in the predicate (the indirect object left in the predicate will almost always be preceded by *to, for, at,* or *of*). For this exercise, select the six pattern 6 sentences from the previous exercise and rewrite them as passives. For three of them, make the indirect object the subject; for the other three make the direct object the subject:

Example: Dorothy wrote him a note.

    a. He was written a note [by Dorothy].
    b. A note was written to him [by Dorothy].

Expanding the Structures

These, then, are the six basic sentence patterns. We're calling these six patterns the basic "structures of expansion" because each can be expanded—built up from inside—by one or more of three methods.

The first method, called *compounding,* simply involves coordinating structures at any point in the sentence. Take, for example, the following (pattern 5) sentence:

Linda bought bonds.

We could introduce a structure of coordination in the subject slot:

Linda and Billie bought bonds

or in the verb slot:

Linda bought and sold bonds

or in the object slot:

Linda bought stocks and bonds

or in all three slots:

Linda and Billie bought and sold stocks and bonds.

The second method of expanding these basic structures involves what are called *modifiers*. More specifically, it involves what we'll call restrictive (or bound) modifiers, as opposed to nonrestrictive (or free) modifiers, a distinction we'll define later. Let's expand another sentence, this time by the use of bound modifiers. Of the following five sentences, the first provides the basic sentence pattern, the remaining four providing information to be added as modifiers:

a. The student transplanted the grapes.
b. The student was in high school.
c. The student had worked for us last summer.
d. The transplanting was hurried.
e. The grapes were wilting.

- The high-school student who had worked for us last summer hurriedly transplanted the wilting grapes.

The third method of expanding a basic sentence pattern involves *nominalizing* an entire sentence to fit the noun slot in a basic pattern. For example, in the *a* (pattern 2) sentence that follows, the subject slot, marked by X, is filled with the information from the *b* sentence.

a. X is true.
b. Josh said [SOMETHING].

- What Josh said is true.

These, then, are the three methods of expanding the basic patterns: compounding (coordination), modifying, and nominalizing. Since we have had a great deal of practice with compounding already (under "Structures of Coordination"), we won't treat it further here. Here we'll treat modifying and nominalizing in greater detail.

Expanding with Modifiers

The most common way to expand a basic pattern is to add restrictive modifiers. Modifiers can be added to a noun unit (subject, subject complement, object, indirect object, etc.). Modifiers can also be added to a verb. In fact modifiers can be added to any unit in a sentence—even to the modifiers themselves. Look what we might do to expand the subject of this very simple pattern 5 sentence:

The dog chased the cat.

Let's begin by adding to our basic pattern 5 sentence the information from the following sentences:

The dog was huge.
The dog was vicious.
The dog was the neighbor's.

First of all, if we delete all the redundant information, we'll be left with only three modifiers—*huge*, *vicious*, and *neighbor's*—which we can add between *the* and *dog*. But second, we'll notice that we can't add the modifiers in just any order we choose. What makes only one of the following sequences an adequate combination of the four sentences above?

a. The huge neighbor's vicious dog chased the cat.
b. The vicious neighbor's huge dog chased the cat.
c. The neighbor's huge, vicious dog chased the cat.

And which one of the following two sequences seems to deliver more accurately the information in the four sentences?

d. The neighbor's vicious, huge dog chased the cat.
e. The vicious, huge neighbor's dog chased the cat.

Exercise 12.9

You will find in the list that follows six sets of sentences. The first sentence in each set will represent one of the six basic patterns. The additional sentences will contain modifiers intended to expand the basic pattern. On a separate sheet of paper combine the sentences in each set so that the result accurately represents the information given. If you can, name the basic sentence pattern each set represents.

Example:
a. Two pies were cooling.
b. The pies were cherry.
c. The pies were freshly baked.
d. The cooling was on the counter.
e. The counter was in the kitchen.

- Two freshly baked cherry pies were cooling on the kitchen counter. (pattern 1)

or

- Two freshly baked cherry pies were cooling on the counter in the kitchen. (pattern 1)

1. *a.* The boy gave the rope a tug.
   b. The boy was terrified.
   c. The boy was five years old.
   d. The rope was frayed.
   e. The tug was with both hands.
2. *a.* The kitten was asleep.
   b. The kitten was a calico.
   c. My father had found the kitten in the woodpile.
   d. The kitten was in the living room.
   e. The kitten was behind the wood stove.
3. *a.* Stock prices rose.
   b. The rise was sharp.
   c. The rise was yesterday.
   d. The rise was in heavy trading.
   e. The stock prices were on the New York Stock Exchange.
4. *a.* *Homo erectus* made axes.
   b. This making of axes occurred over a million years ago.
   c. The axes were for use by hand.
   d. The axes were made from flakes.
   e. The flakes were of obsidian.
   f. The flakes were struck from a core.
5. *a.* The women became shareholders.
   b. There were three women.
   c. Their share holding was in an enterprise.
   d. The women were recently divorced.
   e. The enterprise was data processing.
6. *a.* The party was at a beach.
   b. The party honored the winners.
   c. The winners had won scholarships.
   d. The scholarships were for full tuition.
   e. The scholarships were for four years.
   f. The beach was a few miles north of Malibu.

Restrictive and Nonrestrictive Modifiers

At the beginning of our discussion of structures of expansion it was noted that to understand the concept "structures of expansion" one had to be able to see sentences *a* and *b* as saying essentially the same thing:

a. That guy loves that student.

b. That red-headed Irish guy I introduced you to at Jeanne's party last week really loves that little exchange student from Poland.

And we have just seen that we make *a* into *b* by adding modifiers. Now it's time to see why some modifiers (such as the ones we just looked at) expand a structure and some don't. To do so, we go back to two other sentences we looked at earlier, sentences we noted as saying essentially *different* things:

c. I gave that box of toys to my neighbor who has six kids.

d. I gave that box of toys to my neighbor, who has six kids.

The first thing to be clear on is that sentences *c* and *d* do *not* represent a right way to punctuate and a wrong way to punctuate. They represent two correctly punctuated sentences saying two different things. The distinction is subtle. In fact, many otherwise excellent writers still stumble over this distinction, traditionally labeled *restrictive and nonrestrictive modification*.

Perhaps the easiest way to explain the difference is to share a story (and to ask you to recall a similar story you might share):

I had acquaintances, husband and wife, who had the same name (first and last, as you might guess), at least the same spoken name. He spelled his *Gene* and she spelled hers *Jeanne*, but that only helped when you wrote them.

Still, most of the time there was no confusion. When she answered the door and you asked, "Is Gene in?" she didn't have to ask if you meant her. Most of the time (as in so much of our communication) *context* resolved the meaning. *Context* includes the actual physical situation (you don't ask *about* Jeanne if you're talking *to* her) and includes the surrounding words ("Did Jeanne finish her quilt yet?").

And yet sometimes help was needed. If I were to say to a friend, "I wonder why Jeanne wasn't in church today," the friend might well ask for clarification:

"Who wasn't there—*boy* Gene or *girl* Jeanne?" (or "*big* Gene or *little* Jeanne?" or "Gene with a *G* or Jeanne with a *J*?").

The simple point is this: when we use a term (a word or phrase—even a proper noun) to refer to a person or thing or action or whatever, there's always the potential for ambiguity—always the chance the person we're speaking or writing to will not understand the term to mean what we want it to mean. And so we try to lessen that ambiguity by adding to the term (expanding the structure) till its meaning is clear.

If a boy and a girl are playing on the swings at the park, I can say to a woman looking at them, "The boy is my son." But if there are *two* boys and a girl, I have to add something, a *restrictive* modifier: "The boy *on the right* is my son." And if there are two boys *on the right*, I have to add something else: "The boy *in the striped shirt* is my son." I have to expand the term (through restrictive modifiers) until, given the setting (the physical context), it can refer to one individual only.

But let's back up a notch, to the situation where there were two boys but only one on the right. "The boy on the right" would identify my son. But I might want to add *additional* information: I might want to add that he's in the striped shirt, simply to help the woman I'm addressing to locate him. Here's the problem. The modifier "on the right" identifies my son, *restricts* the term "the boy" to only one possibility: "The boy on the right." So any additional modifiers I add are *redundant* in terms of identifying *the boy;* he's already identified (restricted) to *the boy on the right.* We can still add these redundant modifiers, but we have to set them off with punctuation, as *nonrestrictive* modifiers:

"The boy on the right—the one in the striped shirt—is my son."

Thus, we have a precise tool for *restricting* our term (by expanding it through unpunctuated modification) to exactly the right point. When we've reached that point, any *additional* modifiers are *nonrestrictive*, to be set off by punctuation.

Now, let's look at sentences *c* and *d* once again:

c. I gave that box of toys to my neighbor who has six kids.
d. I gave that box of toys to my neighbor, who has six kids.

Essentially what is the distinction separating *c* from *d?* The distinction is that in *c* the *who* clause is part of a structure of expansion, while in *d* it is not. In *c* the writer (or speaker) assumes that the audience doesn't know who is being referred to by the term *my neighbor* till it is expanded by the modifier *who has six kids—that* neighbor, the one with the six kids. In *d*, on the other hand, the writer (or speaker) assumes that the audience knows who is being referred to by *my neighbor.* The *who* clause simply gives additional information about that neighbor, in this case *why* the writer gave the neighbor the box of toys (because he has six kids).

This explanation is bound to be confusing at first. (For more than a quarter century now, I have been teaching students to recognize the difference between restrictive and nonrestrictive modifiers, and they're always confused at first. I like to think it's because the distinction is so subtle rather than because I'm a lousy teacher.) So let's practice it, with a number of examples.

The rule is that we keep expanding our structure till it is restricted to *one, identified*. Then we close it off with a mark of punctuation before we add any more modification. How do these sentences conform to that rule?

> *e.* His mother who loves flowers is building a greenhouse.
> *f.* His mother, who loves flowers, is building a greenhouse.

Who is building the greenhouse—his mother or his mother who loves flowers? The chances are that he has only the one mother, so we don't need the modifier *who loves flowers* to tell us which mother we're talking about. If we don't need the modifier, we should set it off from our structure of expansion with a pair of punctuation marks. Of course, if two (or more) women can be referred to as *his mother*, then we'll need to expand the structure till it refers to only one. In that case the *who* clause should be part of the structure of expansion.

Notice how that expansion to clarify *which* mother has been accomplished in the three sentences below. And notice, now, that the *who* clause can be kept out of the structures of expansion.

> *g.* His stepmother, who loves flowers, is building a greenhouse.
> *h.* His adoptive mother, who loves flowers, is building a greenhouse.
> *i.* His mother-in-law, who loves flowers, is building a greenhouse.

Now, imagine a case where this *he* we're talking about has more than one mother-in-law (I've had two myself). *His mother-in-law* could now refer to two women. If one loved flowers and one didn't, *who loves flowers* could be used to expand the structure *his mother-in-law* till it referred to only one of them, the one who loved flowers:

> *j.* His mother-in-law who loves flowers is building a greenhouse.

In *j, his mother-in-law who loves flowers* is being differentiated from his other mother-in-law, who, apparently, doesn't love flowers.

Exercise 12.10

Following are ten pairs of sentences, differing only in the amount of information in their structures of expansion. Each pair of sentences is followed by one or more questions. On a separate sheet of paper copy down each pair of sentences (being especially careful to copy the punctuation exactly). Then answer each question.

1. *a.* He searched for his meerschaum pipe which his children had given him last Christmas.
   b. He searched for his meerschaum pipe, which his children had given him last Christmas.

   - Which sentence, *a* or *b,* implies that he has only one meerschaum pipe?

2. *a.* Mohammed Ali's seventh defense of his title against Cleveland Williams featured "The Greatest" at the top of his form.
   b. Mohammed Ali's seventh defense of his title (against Cleveland Williams) featured "The Greatest" at the top of his form.

   - Which sentence says that Mohammed Ali defended his title seven times against Cleveland Williams alone?
   - Which sentence says that the seventh time Ali defended his title the fight happened to be against Cleveland Williams?
   - Sentence 2b actually expresses the facts. What are they?

3. *a.* Thank you for your inquiry about our network show "Lotsa Luck."
   b. Thank you for your inquiry about our network show, "Lotsa Luck."

   - The manager of an NBC-affiliate station wrote one of those sentences but should have written the other. Which sentence implies that the affiliate carries only one network show?
   - "Lotsa Luck" is actually one of many network shows the affiliate carries. Which structure of expansion tells us that?

4. *a.* Debby collected fifteen dollars more than any other girl in her scout troop.
   b. Debby collected fifteen dollars—more than any other girl in her scout troop.

   - Which sentence credits Debby with collecting a grand total of fifteen dollars?
   - Which sentence doesn't tell us how much Debby collected altogether?
   - Which sentence tells us that Debby's total was fifteen dollars higher than the next highest total?

5. *a.* And the Yankees who had looked bad all season dropped their seventh straight to the California Angels.
   b. And the Yankees, who had looked bad all season, dropped their seventh straight, to the California Angels.

- Sentence 5a appeared in print. The other one should have. Can you determine the differences in meaning? Look at the difference that setting off the "to" prepositional phrase makes as well as the difference setting off the "who" clause makes.

6. *a.* The movie *Rambo* was that summer's smash hit.
   b. The movie, *Rambo*, was that summer's smash hit.

- Which of these sentences implies that the context has already been narrowed so that the term *The movie* can refer to only one movie?
- Which of these sentences implies that the term *The movie* can refer to any number of movies and must be expanded till it refers to only one?

7. *a.* Iowa was the twenty-ninth state to enter the Union on 28 December 1846.
   b. Iowa was the twenty-ninth state to enter the Union—on 28 December 1846.

- Which sentence implies that Iowa and at least twenty-eight other states entered the union the same day?
- Which sentence implies that Iowa was not necessarily the twenty-ninth state to enter the Union?
- Which sentence says that Iowa was in fact the twenty-ninth state to enter the Union and that it did so 28 December 1846?
- Which sentence is true?

8. *a.* At her death at age ninety-two she left an estate worth three million dollars.
   b. At her death, at age ninety-two, she left an estate worth three million dollars.

- Since this lady died only once, which sentence do we choose to state the facts?

9. *a.* Other lesser historians have made similar observations.
   b. Other, lesser, historians have made similar observations.

- The historians mentioned so far in the article that this sentence was taken from were Edward Gibbon, Oswald Spengler, and Arnold Toynbee—three of the world's most eminent historians. Which sentence above must we choose if we don't want to imply that these three men were "lesser historians"?

10. *a.* The present quarters are available through January, but the head of the clinic is actively seeking other more permanent quarters.

   b. The present quarters are available through January, but the head of the clinic is actively seeking other, more permanent, quarters.

   ● Context should provide you all the information you need to determine which structure states the facts. Which is it?

Earlier we looked at one sort of relative clause—the cause/effect *which* clause. Now we'll look at several other sorts of relative clauses. Although all but one are capable of serving either as restrictive or nonrestrictive modifiers, they are illustrated here as restrictive modifiers only. Later we'll see which one serves only as a restrictive modifier.

Exercise 12.11

Following are ten pairs of base clauses. Each pair has been combined in such a way that the *b* base becomes a restrictive relative clause embedded in the *a* base. Using these ten sets for your model and using the same relative words, write your own ten pairs of base clauses and then combine them so that the *b* base becomes a relative clause in the *a* base. At times the relative word is enclosed in brackets, to show that it can be omitted.

1. a. The lady refuses to leave a message
   b. The lady keeps calling for Ralph

   ● The lady who keeps calling for Ralph refuses to leave a message.

2. a. I bought the book
   b. You told me about the book

   ● I bought the book [that] you told me about.

3. a. The garage is raising its monthly fee
   b. I park my car at the garage

   ● The garage where I park my car is raising its monthly fee.

4. a. The reason isn't clear
   b. You didn't get the job for some reason

   ● The reason [why] you didn't get the job isn't clear.

5. a. The teacher was Ms. Taylor
   b. I liked the teacher best

   ● The teacher [whom/that] I liked best was Ms. Taylor.

6. *a*. The man is here to pick up the five pounds of Brie
   b. The man's wife ordered the five pounds of Brie

   ● The man whose wife ordered the five pounds of Brie is here to pick it up.

7. *a*. The police found the crowbar
   b. The burglars gained entry by means of the crowbar

   ● The police found the crowbar by means of which the burglars gained entry.

8. *a*. They are the people
   b. He was last seen with the people

   ● They are the people [that] he was last seen with.

   or

   ● They are the people with whom he was last seen.

9. *a*. This is the time
   b. Judith promised to be here at this time

   ● This is the time [when] Judith promised to be here.

10. *a*. The two passengers survived the crash
    b. The two passengers were wearing seat belts

    ● The two passengers who were wearing seat belts survived the crash.

Exercise 12.12

We saw earlier (Exercise 11.6) that subordinate clauses could sometimes be reduced to predicate phrases. The same is true of relative clauses (both restrictive and nonrestrictive). By deleting the relative word and the tense marker from the last sentence of the previous exercise, we reduce the relative clause to a predicate phrase:

The two passengers [who were] wearing seatbelts survived the crash.

Five sentences containing relative clauses as restrictive or nonrestrictive modifiers appear in the following list. Rewrite the sentences, reducing (by deletion of the relative word and the tense marker) the relative clause to a predicate phrase.

Example: The serotonin research which was begun at M.I.T. has yielded significant results.

The serotonin research begun at M.I.T. has yielded significant results.

1. Shuler, who was cited for contempt of court, spent several days in jail.
2. The package that was left in the taxi contained several legal documents.
3. Talbot, who is a close friend of the Mayor, refused to comment.
4. The courts ruled that testimony that is given under duress is inadmissible.
5. Policyholders who drive more than 15,000 miles a year must pay a higher premium.

In careful writing a relative *that* clause is always restrictive (always part of the structure of expansion). And, as the following two examples show, a *that* clause can refer to a human or a nonhuman:

a. The apples that are spoiled should be thrown out.
b. The children that were exposed to measles should be observed carefully for the next few days.

If we make a *that* clause nonrestrictive, we have to substitute another relative word for *that*—*which* if the word referred to designates a nonhuman, *who*** (or, very rarely, *whom*) if it designates a human:

c. These apples, which are spoiled, should be thrown out. [*All* the apples referred to here are spoiled; we're not trying to sort spoiled from nonspoiled here, as we are in sentence *a*.]
d. These children, who were exposed to measles, should be observed carefully for the next few days. [*All* the children referred to here have been exposed to measles.]

Exercise 12.13

Following are four sentences containing (restrictive) *that* clauses. On a separate sheet of paper rewrite each sentence so that the *that* clause is nonrestrictive (is headed by *which* or *who* and is set off by punctuation). Be prepared to state the difference in meaning brought about by the change from restrictive to nonrestrictive.

Example: He threw a rock at the dog that had been tipping over his garbage can.
He threw a rock at the dog, which had been tipping over his garbage can.

In the first sentence the *that* clause tells which dog he threw a rock at. In the second sentence the *which* clause doesn't point out which dog he threw the rock at. (The assumption is that we *know* which dog.) It merely suggests to us *why* he threw the rock.

* Of course, *which* and *who* occur in restrictive clauses also.

1. The two teachers that had gone to Europe for the summer returned refreshed.
2. He searched his pockets for the letter that his wife had asked him to mail.
3. The snake that had just shed its skin was coiled in the center of the cage.
4. He spoke warmly to the girl that smiled at him.

Exercise 12.14

Following are ten sentences, most of which require punctuation to keep from misleading the reader. Punctuate to show nonrestrictive modifiers and be prepared to state the difference in meaning your punctuation makes. Be sure you *don't* set off modifiers that *shouldn't* be set off. For some sentences, hints have been provided by added comment or question.

1. Many aliens who are in the United States illegally are afraid to return to their native country where their lives may well be in danger.

   (*Q:* Are *all* aliens in this country illegally? If not, we don't want to imply that they are by closing the structure of expansion too soon.)
   (*Q:* Does each alien have more than one native country? If not, we don't want to expand the structure *native country* with a restrictive modifier.)

2. They fixed up the spare bedroom for his mother whose disability checks had been discontinued.

   (Assume that he has only one mother.)

3. Romina who is twenty-two is married to Italian pop singer Al Bano.

4. Lacovara's use of the term "definitively" was a subtle reminder that Nixon had once pledged to obey a "definitive" decision of the Supreme Court in the original tapes fight waged by Jaworski's predecessor Archibald Cox.

   (There was only one original tapes fight and Jaworski had only one predecessor. The word *term* has not been limited by context to one term, so we have to expand it with a restrictive modifier.)

5. I acknowledge the help I received from my friend Bill Strong who read the book before publication and made valuable suggestions.

   (Assume I have more than one friend. Assume also that only one of my friends is named Bill Strong.)

6. Only once in this quarter have the Rams been in 49er territory.

   (Assume that the football game is three quarters old and that the Rams have been in 49er territory a total of seven times in the game.)

7. Only once in this quarter have the Rams been in 49er territory.

(Assume that the football game is three quarters old and that the Rams have been in 49er territory only once in the entire game.)

(For the following three, explain why you did or did not set off the modifiers.)

8. Toward the edge of the woods where the original farmhouses had stood one could see three ancient apple trees overrun with blackberry vines.

9. The new drug is being given to AIDS victims who don't respond to other treatments.

10. She cleaned all the rooms except his study which she left for him to clean.

We have seen how our six basic sentence patterns can be expanded by compounding:

Linda bought bonds.
Linda and Billie bought and sold stocks and bonds.

And we have seen how those same six patterns can be expanded by the addition of restrictive modifiers:

The student transplanted the grapes.
The high school student who had worked for us last summer
hurriedly transplanted the wilting grapes.

Now it's time to look at the third way we can expand our six basic patterns: the way usually called "nominalization."

Expanding by Nominalization

Nominalization is a device that allows us to make all or part of a base clause into a nounlike unit—one that will fit any of the noun slots in our six basic patterns. For example, the pattern 2 sentence

a. That is ridiculous

uses the single word *that* to serve as the subject—a noun, or nominal, function. But what about this sentence?

b. What he claims is ridiculous.

Note that sentence *b* has the same basic pattern as sentence *a*. But the one-word subject of *a* is a three-word subject in *b*. And the three words are not a noun and its modifiers; rather, they are the units of a full base clause: He claims [SOMETHING]. In other words, sentence *b* comprises two full base clauses—

> *X* is ridiculous
> He claims [SOMETHING]

—that have been made into one by nominalizing the second base clause and inserting it into the subject slot of the first.

Here are some examples of different ways of nominalizing. See if you can determine what function—subject, object, complement, and so on—the nominalized unit is performing in each case.

1. a. The coach knew *X*
    b. We had stayed up late

The coach knew [that] we had stayed up late.

2. a. The coach knew *X*
    b. We had stayed up late [FOR SOME REASON]

The coach knew why we had stayed up late.

3. a. *X* bothered Linda
    b. Gavin had told Linda [SOMETHING]

What Gavin had told her bothered Linda.
                or
What Gavin had told Linda bothered her.

4. a. The doctor asked *X*
    b. I had been feeling [A CERTAIN WAY]

The doctor asked how I had been feeling.

5. a. He was arrested for *X*
    b. He carried a concealed weapon

He was arrested for carrying a concealed weapon.

6. a. *X* can be very trying
    b. [SOMEONE] gives a dog a bath

Giving a dog a bath can be very trying.
                or
To give a dog a bath can be very trying.

7. a. We considered *X*
    b. Darren was capable of conducting the interview

We considered Darren capable of conducting the interview.

8. *a.* He wanted X
   b. They would leave him alone

He wanted them to leave him alone.

9. *a.* She asked X
   b. She would see the document

She asked to see the document.

10. *a.* The fact X impressed me
    b. Tina had plumbed the entire bathroom by herself

The fact that Tina had plumbed the entire bathroom by herself impressed me.

In the exercise that follows you will be asked to nominalize the *b* sentence and put it in the *a* sentence at the place marked by X. Rather than forcing you to learn grammatical terminology for the various sorts of nominalization you will do, the exercises supply one or more model sentences to guide you.

Exercise 12.15

Following are five pairs of sentences, an *a* sentence, with an X marking the place a nominal (nounlike) unit will go, and a *b* sentence, which will become that nominal and fill the place in *a*. In this exercise the *b* sentence *as a whole*—with or without minor changes—will be placed in the X slot. To nominalize *b* you will use *that*, *whether*, or *if*. With *whether* and *if* the *b* must be changed from a question to an assertion. Write your answers on a separate piece of paper.

Examples:

a. Russian authorities claimed X
b. The Korean Airlines jet was on a spy mission

Russian authorities claimed [that] the Korean Airlines jet was on a spy mission.

a. The question is X
b. Do we have enough fuel left?

The question is whether we have enough fuel left.*

1. *a.* It depends on X.
   b. Was the package insured?

   [whether]

2. *a.* It is a shame X.
   b. You weren't at the party.

   [that]

* Two things to note: (1) Though *b* is a question, when it is nominalized by *whether* or *if*, the question mark disappears. (2) Many people say "whether or not," which, though redundant, is perfectly acceptable.

   3. *a.* X is a shame.   [that]
      b. You weren't at the party.

   4. *a.* She asked X.   [if]
      b. Was everyone comfortable?

   5. *a.* The President wondered X.   [whether]
      b. Did he have support in
         the Senate sufficient to
         pass the measure?

Exercise 12.16

Following are eight sentences, four of which include an indirect question, four of which include a direct question. On a separate sheet of paper rewrite each sentence, changing the indirect question to direct, the direct to indirect. Note carefully the use of quotation marks, capitalization, and punctuation in sentences 5–8 before you change 1–4. Note also that certain verbs and pronouns might have to be changed too.

Examples: *a.* He asked why I was late.   [indirect question]
              a1. He asked, "Why were you late?"   [direct question]

               b. "When will they return?" she asked.   [direct]
              b1. She asked when they would return.   [indirect]

   1. The guard asked what we were doing there.
   2. Lydia asked whether Sam had seen the movie.
   3. I asked who had taken the message.
   4. Jim asked Nancy if she'd like to go home then.
   5. He asked, "Where have they been staying?"
   6. Martha called, "Has anyone seen my keys?"
   7. "Did Edna leave?" he wondered.
   8. "Why haven't you finished?" Steve demanded to know.

Exercise 12.17

The following are eight pairs of sentences—an *a* sentence, with an X marking a missing nominal, and a *b* sentence, to be nominalized and used to replace the X. On a separate sheet of paper, write out the fully nominalized sentence.

Example: *a.* X proved difficult   Funding the program proved
               b. [SOMEONE] funds the   difficult.
                  program

   1. *a.* We enjoyed X
      b. We swam along the canal

2. *a.* X was her favorite job
   b. She fed the calves
3. *a.* X can be traumatic
   b. One changes high schools in one's senior year
4. *a.* X is a treacherous game
   b. [SOMEONE] runs those rapids in a canoe
5. *a.* They tried X
   b. They would stop the hemorrhaging with pressure bandages
6. *a.* X enabled Denzel to pay off his education loans
   b. Denzel worked two jobs
7. *a.* X should be every human being's first concern
   b. [EVERYONE] removes nuclear weapons from this planet
8. *a.* Kate gave X a try
   b. Kate ran the ten-kilometer race

Exercise 12.18

In the previous exercise, the *b* sentences were nominalized as *-ing* phrases and inserted in the *a* sentences:

a. X proved difficult	Funding the program proved difficult.
b. [SOMEONE] funds the program	

Many of these sentences would also work if the *b* sentence were nominalized as an infinitive phrase:

a. X proved difficult	To fund the program proved difficult.
b. [SOMEONE] funds the program	

Some of those sentences also allow an *It* transformation:

It proved difficult to fund the program.

On a separate sheet of paper, redo Exercise 12.17, this time replacing the *-ing* phrase with an infinitive (*to*) phrase wherever possible. (With the first sentence, the infinitive will not work with the verb *enjoyed*, but it will with another verb with a similar meaning.) Try the *It* transformation also wherever possible.

Exercise 12.19

Following are twelve pairs of sentences, an *a* sentence, with an X marking a missing nominal, and a *b* sentence, to be nominalized (as a relative clause) and used to replace X. The relative word needed to replace the word or words capitalized in the *b* sentence has been included in brackets.

At times, word order in the *b* sentence must be changed as part of the nominalizing process. Don't be afraid to experiment.

On a separate sheet of paper, combine the *a* and *b* sentences so that the nominalized *b* sentence (as a relative-clause nominal) replaces the *X* in *a*. Some combinations allow the same *It* transformation you used in the previous exercise.

Examples:

a. Iris wondered *X*
b. They had left FOR SOME REASON—[why]

Iris wondered why they had left.

a. *X* was never determined
b. She had left in SOMEONE'S car—[whose]

Whose car she had left in was never determined.

or

In whose car she had left was never determined.

or

It was never determined whose car she had left in.

1. *a.* *X* remained a mystery
   b. Nancy was finding those raspberries SOMEWHERE [where]
2. *a.* Sandy inquired *X*
   b. Her grandmother was feeling SOME WAY [how]
3. *a.* *X* is immaterial
   b. They got home last night SOMETIME [when]
4. *a.* Don asked Denise *X*
   b. SOMEONE was taking her to the dance [who]
5. *a.* I think I know *X*
   b. These are SOMEONE'S woods [whose]
6. *a.* *X* was obvious
   b. They were referring to SOMEONE [who, *whom]
7. *a.* The document was free to *X*
   b. SOMEONE wanted one [whoever]
8. *a.* We looked for *X*
   b. The dog had bitten SOMEONE [whoever, *whomever]
9. *a.* Everyone was asking *X*
   b. She was SOMEONE [who]
10. *a.* The police wanted to know *X*
    b. SOMEONE'S car was parked across the sidewalk [whose]
11. *a.* *X* was never explained
    b. These documents were copied FOR SOME REASON [why]
12. *a.* She asked *X*
    b. The dog would be kept in SOMEONE'S house [whose]

* *Whom* or *whomever* is historically correct here but rarely used today, especially in informal writing.

Exercise 12.20

Following are four pairs of sentences, an *a* sentence with a "category" noun, in capital letters, and a *b* sentence, to be nominalized as an included (*that*) clause and inserted after the category noun.

Example:

a. The HOPE soon faded
b. Help would arrive

The hope that help would arrive soon faded.

1. a. His FEAR proved well founded
   b. Schultz would make a power play
2. a. The KNOWLEDGE strengthened her
   b. She had prepared for every contingency
3. a. The FACT absolutely astounds most people
   b. Crickets make their song with the edges of their wings rather than with their legs.
4. a. Your first PRESUPPOSITION is questionable*
   b. The Soviets want war

Exercise 12.21

Following are sets of base clauses representing various nominalizing strategies, some of them illustrating several levels of nominalization. Let each set serve as a model for a sentence you will write. As you examine these models, try to discover the sentence pattern each base represents and the sorts of structures they become when nominalized. Also, play with additional variants whenever you think of them.

1. a. We considered X
   b. The plan was unworkable

   We considered the plan unworkable.

2. a. Edna found X
   b. Sam was a pain in the neck

   Edna found Sam [to be] a pain in the neck.

3. a. Have you heard X
   b. The Libyans are claiming SOMETHING

   Have you heard what the Libyans are claiming?

4. a. X is a mystery
   b. She was born SOME-WHERE

   Where she was born is a mystery.

5. a. Despite X, he was the most productive worker
   b. He was old
   c. He was disabled

   Despite his age and his disability, he was the most productive worker.

* Since the context allows for only one first presupposition, the *that* clause is nonrestrictive and must be set off by commas or other paired marks of punctuation.

6. a. X disappointed them
   b. She was reluctant to discuss the letter
   c. She was reluctant to discuss the conversation

Her reluctance to discuss the letter or the conversation disappointed them.

7. a. I wonder X
   b. He knows X [?]
   c. He is doing SOMETHING

I wonder if he knows what he is doing.

8. a. She found X
   b. X was exciting
   c. She lived in Reno

She found living in Reno [to be] exciting.

9. a. X made sense
   b. He told SOMEONE SOMETHING
   c. SOMEONE would listen

What he told whoever would listen made sense.

10. a. X proved impossible
    b. SOMEONE would get X
    c. The President would acknowledge X
    d. We are partially responsible

To get the President to acknowledge that we are partially responsible proved impossible.

Conclusion

Certainly we can't claim to have looked at all the nominalizing techniques the English language allows—or of all the subtleties of relations or coordination or punctuation or chunking for that matter. But it wasn't the goal of this text to be exhaustive. The goal was merely to provide you with the most basic tools for understanding how complex discourse is put together. The goal was to get you started, to make you more aware of how the writers whose discourse you will read have solved their problems (or haven't), which will improve your chances of solving similar problems. *Generating Prose* is intended to give you the foundation you need to learn how to write well. That learning will go on for years, all your life I hope. (I have been writing for forty-five years, and I still learn each time I read or write anything.)

As a closing assignment, let's return to *Northbound*, Gregory Strachov's watercolor painting, which you analyzed as a structure in Essay Assignment Two. The purpose of this final writing assignment is to allow you to put to work toward a single goal everything we've talked about in this text.

❖———————————————————————————❖

Essay Assignment Eight
A Synthesizing Essay:
Re-viewing *Northbound*

Northbound, the painting reproduced on the cover of your text, was painted by Gregory Strachov shortly after his father's death. The setting is the coast of Maine, a stretch of shore between Bar Harbor and Seal Cove, a place Strachov told me he often visits at times of deep introspection. He said of the setting, "I went there after my father died, in order to deal with his death, to understand his death. . . . While I was painting *Northbound*, issues of death and resurrection dominated my thoughts."

With these facts in mind, look again at the painting. Look for expressions of death and of resurrection, of despair and hope, of depression and affirmation. This assignment will involve you in a special sort of whole/quality analysis, where you will be looking not merely for sensory components (our focus in depictive writing) but also, and more importantly, for emotional components or qualities. As you explore the topic, consider the qualities you normally associate with depression or gloom. Here are some I think of: *dark, heavy, grey, low, oppressed, down, beneath, bleak, hushed, cold, directionless, dismal,* and *corporeal*. Consider also the qualities you associate with hope and affirmation. I think of *bright, colorful, light, uplifting, floating, warm, determined, goal oriented, structured, new,* and *spiritual*.

Notice how Strachov has expressed both sets of qualities. Consider also such opposites (perhaps complements?) as the eternal and the momentary, earth and sky, the many and the solitary. And when you explore these concepts, remind yourself that you are juggling abstractions, which is even tougher than juggling limes.

Finally, in a carefully developed theme, using your best techniques of structure analysis, of exposition, and of persuasion, argue whether *Northbound* is basically an expression of despair or of hope.

Index